A Hazardous Materials Glossary for Emergency Responders

Street Smart Chemistry Volume 2

By

Barry N. Lindley MS

And

Wayne C. Appleton PhD

Acronyms and Glossary of Terms

A

"A" End of a railcar- A term used to identify locations on a railcar, being the end opposite the "B" or Brake end. Used in conjunction with "L" or "R" to designate either the left or right side of the car.

AAR - Association of American Railroads. An industry trade association whose purposes include the promotion of railroad interests and the standardization and coordination of operating and mechanical activities within the railroad industry.

Abrasive - Something that grinds down or wears away an object.

Absolute – Composition -A chemical substance relatively free of impurities—such as "absolute alcohol"

Absolute-Temperature Temperature on the Kelvin Scale where 0°C is 273°K

Absorb - To soak up or drink in.

Absorbed Dose - The amount of energy imparted by nuclear radiation to unit mass of absorbing material. The unit is the rad.

Absorption - The process by which a chemical moves into plants & animals. The passing of a substance into the circulatory system of the body or used specifically to refer to entry of toxicants through the skin.

AC US military designator for hydrogen cyanide (HCN).

ACAA - Automatic Chemical Agent Alarm

ACADA - Automatic Chemical Agent Detector/Alarm – An automated system to detect chemical warfare agents, the ACADA may be in a fixed location or mobile or even hand-carried.

Acaricide - A substance that is toxic to mites and ticks. A miticide is an acaricide.

Acetylcholine - A chemical released by certain nerves that stimulates a muscle, gland, or another nerve. This is one of a number of neurotransmitters in the body that carry "messages" from nerves to other organs.

Acetylcholinesterase - An enzyme (a protein produced in the cells) that stops the action of acetylcholine by destroying it. This action occurs as soon as acetylcholine has produced a muscle contraction or stimulated a gland or nerve. Nerve agents combine with acetylcholinesterase to prevent it from destroying acetylcholine; acetylcholine accumulates in excess and continues tostimulate the muscle, gland, or nerve.

ACGIH - American Conference of Governmental Industrial Hygienists. Develops and publishes TLV values.

Acid - An inorganic or organic compound that –
    1) reacts with metals and human tissue;
    2)material that has a pH less than 7;
    3) neutralizes bases or alkaline material;
    4) reacts with bases to form salts.

Acidosis - pathologic condition resulting from accumulation of acid in, or loss of base from, the blood or body tissues

ACM - Asbestos containing material.

Acne form - resembling acne

Acre - 43,560 square feet.

Acrid - Irritating and bitter odor.

ACTD - Advanced Concept Technology Demonstration

Action Level - A concentration designated in Title 29, Code of Federal Regulations, Part 1910 (29 CFR 1910) for a specific substance, calculated as an 8-hour time-weighted average, which initiates certain required activities such as exposure monitoring and medical surveillance. [Note: For many substances the action level is one-half the Permissible Exposure Limit (PEL.)]

Action Plan - See Incident Action Plan.

Activator - An additive, usually for pesticides, used to increase its efficiency.

Active Ingredient - The active or useful portion of a product which, by itself, can cause the desired effect.

Acute - Of short duration / immediate toxic effects. Acute health effects are those that occur during or immediately after exposure.

Acute Effects - Usually immediate, obvious, short-term responses to exposure to a hazard. They can be localized to one part of the body or they can be systemic.

Acute Exposure - An exposure to a toxic substance which occurs in a short or single time period less than 24 hours.

Acute Toxicity - A term used to describe immediate toxicity. Its use is associated with toxic effects that are severe (e.g., mortality) in contrast to the term "subchronic toxicity," which is associated with toxic effects that are less severe. The term "acute toxicity" is often confused with that of acute exposure. The capacity of a pesticide to cause injury within 24 hours following exposure. LD50 and LC50 are common indicators of the degree of acute toxicity.

Adamsite is a common name for DM, also known as "nausea gas.". DM is the military designator for a vomit agent with the chemical name diphenylaminochloroarsine (also phenarsazine chloride). DM is an irritating agent with rapid onset of rhinorrhea and lacrimation symptoms associated with headache, nausea, and severe vomiting. It is not stocked or used by the US military but has been used in other countries as a "crowd control agent" against civilians protesting government actions and policies.

Additive Effect - A biological response to exposure to multiple chemicals which is equal to the sum of the effects of the individual agents.

Adjuvant - An agent added to a product to improve its activity. This term is frequently used with pesticides.

Adsorb - To collect on the surface of another material.

Adsorption - The process by which materials are held on the surface. The bonding of chemicals to soil particles or other surfaces.

Adulticide - Something toxic to the adult stage of an organism.

Adverse Effect - A biochemical change, functional impairment, or pathological lesion that impairs performance and reduces the ability of the organism to respond to additional challenges.

Adverse Effect Level (AEL) - An exposure level at which there are statistically or biologically significant increases in frequency or severity of deleterious effects between the exposed population and its appropriate control group.

ADW - Agent Defeat Weapon

AEL - Adverse Effect Level; Airborne Exposure Limits

AEGL-1 is the airborne concentration (expressed as parts per million (ppm) or milligram/meter cubed (mg/m3)) of a substance above which it is predicted that the general population, including susceptible individuals, could experience notable discomfort, irritation, or certain asymptomatic, non-sensory effects. However, the effects are not disabling and are transient and reversible upon cessation of exposure.

AEGL-2 is the airborne concentration (expressed as ppm or mg/m3) of a substance above which it is predicted that the general population, including susceptible individuals, could experience irreversible or other serious, long-lasting adverse health effects, or an impaired ability to escape.

AEGL-3 is the airborne concentration (expressed as ppm or mg/m3) of a substance above which it is predicted that the general population, including susceptible individuals, could experience life-threatening health effects or death.

Aerosol - Particles dispersed in a gas (usually air). Examples are fog (liquid particles) and smoke (solid particles). Very fine liquid droplets or dust particles often emitted from a pressurized can or aerosol generating device. Large enough to be filtered from the air. Particle size may vary from 100 to 0.01 microns in diameter.

Agency - An agency is a division of government with a specific function, or a nongovernmental organization (e.g., private contractor, business, etc.) that offers a particular kind of assistance. In ICS, agencies are defined as jurisdictional (having statutory responsibility for incident mitigation) or assisting and/or cooperating (providing resources and/or assistance). (See **Assisting Agency, Cooperating Agency, Jurisdictional Agency, and Multiagency Incident**.)

Agency Dispatch - The agency or jurisdictional facility from which resources are allocated to incidents.

Agency Representative - A person assigned by a primary, assisting, or cooperating Federal, State, local, or tribal government agency or private entity that has been delegated authority to make decisions affecting that agency's or organization's participation in incident management activities following appropriate consultation with the leadership of that agency. Agency Representatives report to the Incident Liaison Officer.

Agent BZ - The chemical 3-quinuclidinyl ester, chemical abstracts service (CAS) registry No. 6581-06-2. BZ is a code designation for a potent psychoactive compound that has a pharmacological action similar to that of other anticholinergic drugs (atropine, scopolamine for example) except that the effects are more severe and longer lasting. It is an incapacitating agent classified as a Class B poison for transportation purposes. It is an odorless, white crystalline solid that in granular form may be compounded with a fuel-oxidizer mix for thermal dissemination.

Agent GA - The chemical Ethyl N,N-dimethylphosphoramidocyanidate, CAS registry No. 77- 81-6, in pure form and in the various impure forms found in storage as well as in industrial, depot, or laboratory operations (synonym = **Tabun**). Agent GA is a nerve agent.

Agent GB - The chemical Isopropyl methylphosphonofluoridate, CAS registry No. 107-44-8, in pure form and in the various impure forms found in storage as well as in industrial, depot, orlaboratory operations (synonym = **Sarin**). Agent GB is a nerve agent.

Agent GD - The chemical Pinacolyl methylphosphonofluoridate, methyl-1, 2, 2-trimethylpropyl ester, CAS registry No. 96-64-0, in pure form and in the various impure forms found in storage as well as in industrial, depot, or laboratory operations (synonym = **Soman**). Agent GD is a nerve agent.

Agent H - Levinstein mustard, CAS registry No. 471-03-4. A mixture of 70 percent bis (2-chloroethyl) sulfide and 30 percent sulfur impurities produced by the Levinstein process. Agent H is a blister agent.

Agent HD - Distilled mustard or bis (2-chloroethyl) sulfide, CAS registry No. 505-60-2. Distilled mustard (HD) is mustard (H) that has been purified by washing and vacuum distillation to reduce sulfur impurities. Agent HD is a blister agent.

Agent HT - A plant-run mixture of 60 percent HD and 40 percent T plus a variety of sulfur contaminants and impurities. T is bis [2-(2-chloroethylthio)ethyl]ether, CAS registry No. 63918- 89-8. T is a sulfur, oxygen and chlorine compound similar in structure to HD. Agent HT is a blister agent.

Agent L, or **Lewisite** – Dichloro- 2-chlorovinyldichloroarsine, CAS registry No. 541-25-3; its chemical formula is C2H2AsCl3. Agent L is a blister agent.

Agent VX - The chemical Phosphonothioic acid, methyl-S-[2-(bis(1-methylethyl)amino)ethyl] 0-ethyl ester, CAS registry No. 50782-69-9, in pure form and in the various impure forms that may be found in storage as well as in industrial, depot, or laboratory operations. Agent VX is a nerve agent that is highly toxic at extremely low exposures.

Agitate - To mix

AICPS - Advanced Integrated Collective Protective System

AIDS- Acquired Immune Deficiency Syndrome

Airbill - a shipping paper prepared from a bill of lading that accompanies each piece of an air shipment.

Air Inversion - a meteorological condition in the Earth's atmosphere in which the temperature of the air some distance above the Earth's surface is higher than the air temperature of the surface. Normally, air temperatures decrease as altitude increases, such a condition traps air, and releases gases and vapors near the Earth's surface, thus impending their dispersion.

Air Operations Branch Director - The person primarily responsible for preparing and implementing the air operations portion of the Incident Action Plan. Also responsible for providing logistical support to helicopters operating on the incident.

Air reactivity - Air reactivity describes substances that will ignite, decompose or release energy when exposed to the oxygen in air.

Airborne Exposure Limit (AEL) - Personnel working without protection from the inhalation of agent vapors in areas where agent may be present will not be exposed to concentrations exceeding the AEL. The permissible time weighted average airborne exposure concentration for an 8 hour day of a 40 hour week.

Allowable Exposure Limit (AEL)—Some corporations and jurisdictions use this term instead of Airborne Exposure Limit

AIT—Autoignition Temperature- The temperature at which a compound will self-ignite due to decomposition and exothermic bond breaking.

Albuminuria - presence of serum albumin in the urine

ALCM - Air Launched Cruise Missile

Alcohol resistant foam - A firefighting foam that is resistant to "polar" chemicals such as alcohols, ketones and esters which may break down other types of foam.

Aldehydes - Any of various highly reactive compounds typified by acetaldehyde and characterized by the group CHO.

Algae - Simple plants that contain chlorophyll and are photosynthetic.

Algicide - A substance that is toxic to algae.

Alkali or alkaline - A basic substance or material having basic properties. Usually oxides or hydroxides of metals, although ammonia and amines are also alkaline. Alkaline materials are caustic and dissolve human tissue. The pH is greater than 7. A chemical which neutralizes acids forming salts.

Alkyl- an Organic chemical group having only carbon and hydrogens—often named after the non-hydrogen substituent such as Alkyl halides which contain a halogen substituted for one or more hydrogens.

Allergen - A substance that may cause an allergic reaction in people who are sensitive to a particular allergen.

Allocated Resources - Resources dispatched to an incident.

ALOHA®—ALOHA® is the hazard modeling program for the CAMEO® software suite, which is used widely to plan for and respond to chemical emergencies. ALOHA allows you to enter details about a real or potential chemical release, and then it will generate threat zone estimates for various types of hazards. ALOHA can model toxic gas clouds, flammable gas clouds, BLEVEs (Boiling Liquid Expanding Vapor Explosions), jet fires, pool fires, and vapor cloud explosions. The threat zone estimates are shown on a grid in ALOHA, and they can also be plotted on maps in MARPLOT®, Esri's ArcMap, Google Earth, and Google Maps. The red threat zone represents the worst hazard level, and the orange and yellow threat zones represent areas of decreasing hazard. (From the USEPA Website).

All-Risk - Any incident or event, natural or human-caused, which warrants action to protect life, property, environment, public health and safety, and minimize disruption of governmental, social, and economic activities.

Alopecia - baldness; absence of hair from skin areas where it is usually present

Alpha particle - Named after and denoted by the first letter in the Greek alphabet, α, consists of two protons and two neutrons bound together into a particle identical to a helium nucleus, which is produced in the process of alpha decay.

ALS - Advanced Life Support

Alveoli - Microscopic air sac in the lungs where oxygen and carbon dioxide diffusion takes place through the alveolar walls.

Amatol—An explosive consisting of TNT and Ammonium Nitrate.

Ambient - Usual or surrounding conditions. For example, 75°F and 1 atmosphere pressure.

AMEDD - Army Medical Department

AMFO—Also ANFO—A mixture of Ammonium Nitrate and Fuel Oil used as a blasting agent or secondary explosive in construction, mining, etc. ANFO has been used in numerous Improvised Explosive Devices by combatant and terrorist groups ranging from the Middle East to Basque Separatists.

Amine - Any of a class of organic compounds derived from ammonia by replacement of hydrogen with one or more alkyl groups.

Amorphous solid- without definite form, not crystallized. Most polymers are amorphous solids.

Anaphylactoid - resembling an unusual or exaggerated allergic reaction to foreign protein or other substances

Anesthetic- a chemical that induces insensibility to pain, such as chloroform or diethyl ether.

ANFO—Also AMFO—A mixture of Ammonium Nitrate and Fuel Oil used as a blasting agent or secondary explosive in construction, mining, etc. ANFO has been used in numerous Improvised Explosive Devices by combatant and terrorist groups ranging from the Middle East to Basque Separatists.

Anhydride - Compound derived from acidic compounds by removing "water". Materials are water reactive.

Anhydrous - Means dry without water.

Anorexia - lack or loss of appetite for food

Anoxemia - Inadequate oxygenation of the blood.

Anoxia - Lack of oxygen.

Antagonism - The situation in which two chemicals interfere with each other's actions, or one chemical interferes with the action of the other.

Anthelmintic - an agent that is destructive to worms especially of the intestine

Anthrax - A highly lethal infection caused by the bacterium Bacillus anthracis; normally, a disease of livestock that can be transmitted to man by direct contact with or ingestion of contaminated meat, hide, wool, hair, blood, or excreta. In most cases involving humans, the bacteria enters the body through skin wounds and infects the skin. In other cases, the bacteria may be ingested (eaten) or inhaled. Spore inhalation results in the inhalation form of anthrax that is characterized by a human fatality rate of nearly 90 percent. A short period of flu-like symptoms that is followed by respiratory distress; shock and death usually follows within 24 – 36 hours after onset of respiratory distress. Anthrax can be treated with antibiotics, but treatment must be started early to be effective.

Antibiotic - A natural or synthetic substance that inhibits the growth of or destroys microorganisms. Used extensively in the treatment of infectious diseases in plants, animals, and humans.

Anticholinergic - An agent or chemical that blocks or impedes the action of acetylcholine, such as the antidote atropine.

Anticholinesterase - A substance that blocks the action of cholinesterase (acetylcholinesterase), such as nerve agents.

Anticoagulant - A chemical which stops the clotting process in blood.

Antidote - A material administered to an individual who has been exposed to a poison in order to counteract the poison's toxic effects.

Anti-Lewisite - dimercaprol; also called British Anti-Lewisite, or BAL. A chemical developed during World War I to counteract the blister agent Lewisite.

Antimetabolite - a substance that interferes with utilization of an essential metabolite

Antipyretic - an agent that relieves or reduces fever

Anti-siphoning Device - A device attached to the filling hose that prevents backflow or backsiphoning from a spray tank into a water source.

Aphasia - defect or loss of power of expression by or comprehension of speech, writing, or signs

APHIS - Animal and Plant Health Inspection Service

Aphonia - Inability to phonate or produce speech sounds.

Aplasia - Failure of production of cellular products from an organ or tissue, such as blood cells from the bone marrow, after a toxic dose of mustard.

Apnea - Cessation of breathing.

Appearance – What the material looks like; solid, gas, liquid, color, texture, particle size, etc.

Aqueous, aq. - Indicates water is present in the solution.

Aquifer - An underground bed, or layer, of earth, gravel, or porous storage that contains water.

Arachnid - A wingless arthropod with two body regions and four pairs of jointed legs. Spiders, ticks, and mites are in the class Arachnida.

Area Command (Unified Area Command) - An organization established (1) to oversee the management of multiple incidents that are each being handled by an ICS organization or (2) to oversee the management of large or multiple incidents to which several Incident Management Teams have been assigned. Area Command has the responsibility to set overall strategy and priorities, allocate critical resources according to priorities, ensure that incidents are properly managed, and ensure that objectives are met and strategies followed. Area Command becomes Unified Area Command when incidents are multijurisdictional. Area Command may be established at an emergency operations center facility or at some location other than an incident command post.

Argyrosis - poisoning by silver or a silver salt, evidenced by ashen-gray discoloration of skin

Aromatic Hydrocarbons – A material that contains a Benzene or benzene-like structure. An aromatic hydrocarbon (abbreviated as AH) or arene (or sometimes aryl hydrocarbon) is a hydrocarbon with a conjugated cyclic molecular structure that is much more stable than the hypothetical localized structure.

Arrhythmia - any variation from the normal rhythm of the heart beat

Arsenicals - A category of blister agents in which arsenic is the central atom. Although more volatile than mustard agents, they are much more dangerous as liquids than as vapors.

Arteriosclerosis - hardening and thickening of the walls of the smaller arteries

Arthropod - An invertebrate animal characterized by a jointed body and limbs and usually a hard body covering that is molted at intervals. For example, insects, mites, and crayfish are in the phylum Arthropoda.

Asphyxiant - Substance that interferes with oxygenation of tissue with the result of possible suffocation. Chemicals that starve the cells of an individual from the life-giving oxygen needed to sustain metabolism.

Asphyxiation - Injury or death caused by the replacement of oxygen in the environment by another gas or vapor.

Assessment - The evaluation and interpretation of measurements and other information to provide a basis for decision-making.

Assigned Resources - Resources checked in and assigned work tasks on an incident.

Assignments - Tasks given to resources to perform within a given operational period that are based on operational objectives defined in the IAP.

Assistant - Title for subordinates of principal Command Staff positions. The title indicates a level of technical capability, qualifications, and responsibility subordinate to the primary positions. Assistants may also be assigned to unit leaders.

Assisting Agency - An agency or organization providing personnel, services, or other resources to the agency with direct responsibility for incident management. See also Supporting Agency.

Asthenia - lack or loss of strength; weakness

Astringent - causing contraction, usually locally after surface application

Asym - An abbreviation for asymmetrical - referring to a particular arrangement of elements within a chemical molecule.

Ataxia (ataxic) - A staggering or unsteady gait; inability to walk a straight line.

Ataxis - failure of muscular coordination; irregularity of muscular action

Atelectasis - Collapse of the alveoli of the lungs secondary to mucous plugs, foreign bodies, and secretions. Frequently associated with pneumonia, best treated by vigorous coughing and breathing exercises, as well as Positive Pressure Breathing with PEEP.

ATF --The Bureau of Alcohol, Tobacco and Firearms

Atmosphere, atm - Measurement of pressure. 1 atm = 14.7 psi.

Atomic Number - The atomic number of an element, which indicates its place in the periodic table of elements, is the number of protons (positively charged particles) in the nucleus of one ofits atoms. If an atom is electrically neutral, the same number of electrons are present. Forexample, the letter C preceded by a superscript number 12 and a subscript number 6 indicates a carbon atom of atomic mass 12 and atomic number 6, the difference being equal to the number of neutrons present in the nucleus.

Atomic weight - The mass of an element.

Atomize - To break up a liquid into very small, fine droplets so that it is easily spread and settles slowly.

Atropine - An alkaloid obtained from the plant Atropa belladonna. It is used as an antidote for nerve agent poisoning. It inhibits the actions of acetylcholine at the nerve/muscle junction.

Attractant - A substance that attracts a specific species of animal to it. When manufactured to attract pests to traps or poisoned baits, attractants are considered to be pesticides.

Autoignition temperature -AIT- The lowest temperature at which a substance will ignite in air when there is no other ignition source other than temperature.

Auto refrigeration - The process in which a gas is kept at its boiling point, so that any added heat is countered by energy lost from boil off. The gas evaporates and cools off till it reaches its boiling point and is at a steady state where the pool is kept at the boiling point of the gas.

Available Resources - Resources assigned to an incident, checked in, and available for a mission assignment, normally located in a Staging Area.

Avicide - an agent that kills birds

Awareness Level Trained - First responders at the awareness level are those persons who, in the course of their normal duties may be the first on the scene of an emergency involving hazardous materials. First responders at the awareness level are expected to recognize hazardous materials presence, protect themselves, call for trained personnel, and secure the area. (NFPA 472)

B

"B" end of the car. The end on which the hand brake is located.

Background Radiation - Nuclear (or ionizing) radiations arising from within the body and from the surroundings to which individuals are always exposed. The main sources of the natural background radiation are potassium-40 in the body, potassium-40 and thorium, uranium, and their decay products (including radium) present in rocks and soil, and cosmic rays.

Bacteria - Microscopic organisms, some of which are capable of producing diseases in plants and animals. Single-celled organisms that multiply by cell division and can cause disease in humans,plants, or animals. Examples include anthrax, cholera, plague, tularemia, and Q fever.

Bactericide - A substance that is toxic to bacteria.

Bacterium - Any of numerous unicellular microorganisms of the class Schizomycetes, occurring in a wide variety of forms, existing either as free-living organisms or as parasites, and having a wide range of biochemical activity.

Baffle - an intermediate partial bulkhead which reduces the surge effect in a partially loaded tank.

Bait - Something attractive to a target organism which normally contains a toxicant of some kind.

Bait Shyness - The tendency of organisms to avoid bait.

BAL - British anti-Lewisite—A material developed during World War I to counter the blister effects of Lewisite.

Band Application - Application of a pesticide in a strip alongside or around a structure, a portion of a structure or any object.

Bar - A measure of atmospheric pressure 1 Bar=100 kPa (kilopascals) = 14.5 psi

Barrel - 42 US gallons-a measure used mainly for petroleum products

Barrier Application - See band application.

Base - Material that has a pH greater than 7. Reacts with acids to give salts.

Base - The location at which primary Logistics functions for an incident are coordinated and administered. There is only one Base per incident. (Incident name or other designator will be added to the term Base.) The Incident Command Post may be collocated with the Base.

Basic Life Support (CPR) - First aid measures done to assist a victim's breathing and heart action such as cardiopulmonary resuscitation.

BDO - Battle Dress Overgarment

BDU - Battle Dress Uniform

Becquerel -Bq   A modern unit of radioactivity replacing the Curie; the activity of an amount of a radioactive material in which one nucleus decays each second.

Beneficial Insect - An insect that is useful or helpful to humans. Usually insect parasites, predators, pollinators, etc.

Beta particle - High-energy, high-speed electrons or positrons emitted by certain types of radioactive nuclei such as potassium-40. The beta particles emitted are a form of ionizing radiation also known as beta rays. The production of beta particles is termed beta decay.

Bi - Prefix meaning two.

BIDS - Biological Integrated Detection System

Binary Precursors - The component chemicals that combine to produce chemical agents. Binary precursors may be toxic and reactive but are less toxic and more easily stored than the Agent that they react to form when mixed.

Bioaccumulation - increased concentrations of a chemical in an organism compared to the surrounding environment.

Biodegradable - Capable of decomposing quickly through the action of microorganisms.

Biological agent - Living organisms, or the materials derived from them, which cause disease in, or harm, humans, animals, or plants, or cause deterioration of material. Biological agents may be found as liquid droplets, aerosols, or dry powders. A biological agent can be adapted and used as a terrorist weapon, such as anthrax, tularemia, cholera, encephalitis, plague, and botulism. There are three different types of biological agents: bacteria, viruses, and toxins.

Biological Control - The control of certain organisms by the use of their natural enemies, such as predators, parasites or disease.

Biomagnification - The process where one organism accumulates chemical residues in higher concentrations from organisms they consume. The tendency of certain chemicals to become concentrated as they move into and up the food chain.

Blast - The brief and rapid movement of air away from a center of outward pressure, as in an explosion. This term is commonly used to mean explosion, but the two terms should be distinguished.

Blasting Agent - a material that is very insensitive with little probability of accidental ignition. Blasting Agents such as ANFO require a detonator to explode and may burn without explosion if ignited without a blasting cap or other detonator.

Blasting Cap-a small sensitive explosive used to initiate the explosion of a larger and less sensitive explosive

Blepharospasm - A twitching or spasmodic contraction of muscles around the eye; if severe, can lead to closure of the eyes.

BLEVE - An acronym for Boiling Liquid Expanding Vapor Explosion. Materials which BLEVE may cause storage containers and parts of containers to rocket great distances, in many directions. Any liquid may cause a BLEVE. BLEVEs typically occur when a tank or storage container is heated and the pressure inside the tank reaches the "burst pressure" of the structure. See also "Heat Induced Tear"

Blister Agent - A chemical (such as sulfur mustard) that produces local irritation and damage to the skin and mucous membranes that progresses in severity to fluid-filled blisters on skin. This chemical can cause damage by exposure to liquid or vapor inhalation (IH). It can also produce damage to the respiratory tract.

Blood Agent - A blood agent is a toxic chemical agent that affects the body by being absorbed into the blood and prevents the normal transfer of oxygen from the blood to the body tissues, resulting in chemical asphyxiation. The brain, being highly dependent upon a continual source of oxygenation, is especially susceptible. Clinical signs include hyperventilation, which further enhances the dose received, resulting in abrupt cardiovascular collapse. They are fast-acting, potentially lethal poisons that typically manifest at room temperature as volatile colorless gases with a faint odor. Blood agents are typically either cyanide- or arsenic-based

Blow Down Valve -a manually operated valve whose function is to quickly reduce tank pressure to atmospheric pressure.

Blue Flag - A blue signal (flag or sign by day, light by night), displayed at one or both ends of an engine, car or train, indicating that workmen are under, on or about the train or equipment. When thus protected, it must not be coupled or moved. A Blue Flag is used in conjunction with a derailleur to isolate a track while people are working there.

BM/C3I - Battle Management/Command, Control, Communications, and Intelligence

BMD - Ballistic Missile Defense

BMDO - Ballistic Missile Defense Organization

B-NICE - Biological, nuclear, incendiary, chemical, explosive

BOD - Biological Oxygen Demand - amount of oxygen required by bacteria to digest decomposable organic matter under aerobic conditions.

Body Bolster - The transverse members of the underframe over the trucks which transmit the load carried by the longitudinal sill to the trucks through the center plates.

Body Center Plates - A cast or forged steel plate riveted or welded to the body bolster at the car center line, the function of which is to transmit the body bolster load to the trucks through the truck bolster.

Body Side Bearing - A flat settle bearing pad fastened to the body bolster, a standard distance outboard of the center pin hole, the function of which is to support the load of a moving car when variations in track cross level or other train dynamics cause the car to rock transversely on the center plates. A conventional car has four body side bearings (one at each corner).

Boil - To change from a liquid state to a gaseous state.

Boilover - the violent expulsion of oil and froth from a tank due to the rapid expansion of water into steam when the heat wave in the oil reaches the water layer, usually suspended toward the bottom of a tank of heavy or unrefined oil.

Boiling point - Temperature at which the vapor pressure of a liquid equals the atmospheric pressure and boils. A chemical with a low boiling point can boil and evaporate quickly. If a material that is flammable also has a low boiling point, a special fire hazard exists.

Botanical Pesticide - A pesticide produced from chemicals found in plants. Examples are nicotine, pyrethrins, and strychnine.

Botulism - Poisoning by toxin derived from the microorganism Clostridium botulinum.

Bradycardia - slowness of the heartbeat, as evidenced by slowing of pulse rate to less than 60

Branch - The organizational level having functional or geographical responsibility for major aspects of incident operations. A branch is organizationally situated between the section and the division or group in the Operations Section, and between the section and units in the Logistics Section. Branches are identified by the use of Roman numerals or by functional area.

Brand Name - The name, or designation of a specific pesticide product or device made by a manufacturer or formulator. A marketing name.

Breakthrough - When a chemical permeates to the point where it can be detected on the inside of the barrier material.

Breakthrough Time - The time it takes a given chemical to permeate a barrier material.

Broad Spectrum – As applied to pesticides- a product that works over a very wide range or against a large number of organisms.

Bronchoconstriction - Constriction of the bronchial tubes making it difficult to move air in and out of the lungs.

Bronchoconstriction - narrowing of the air passages of the lungs

Bronchopneumonia - Inflammation of the terminal bronchioles and alveoli, causing edema and consolidation of alveoli.

Brucella - A genus of encapsulated, non-motile bacteria (family Brucellaceae) containing short, rod-shaped to coccoid, Gram-negative cells. These organisms are parasitic, invading all animal tissues and causing infection of the genital organs, the mammary gland, and the respiratory and intestinal tracts, and are pathogenic for man and various species of domestic animals. They do not produce gas from carbohydrates. If used as a biological warfare agent, it would move likely be delivered by the aerosol route; the resulting infection would be expected to mimic natural disease.

BTU - A British thermal unit. The amount of heat required changing the temperature of one pound of water one degree Fahrenheit at sea level.

Bubo - Inflammatory swelling of one or more lymph nodes, usually in the groin; the confluent mass of nodes usually suppurates and drains pus.

Bulk Container - a cargo container, such as a tank truck or tank car, used for transporting materials in bulk quantities.

Bubonic Plague - A form of plague characterized by the presence of inflammatory swellings of lymph nodes that first occur at the regional node site closets to the bite of an infected flea.

Bulkhead - a structure used to protect against damage caused by shifting cargo and or to separate loads.

Bulk Plant - that portion of a property where flammable or combustible liquids are received by tank vessel, pipe line, tank cars, or tank vehicle, and are stored or blended in bulk for the purpose of distributing such liquids by tank vessel.

Bulla (Pl. Bullae) - A large blister appearing as a circumscribed area of separation of the epidermis from the subepidermal structure (subepidermal bulla) or as a circumscribed area of separation of epidermal cells (intraepidermal bulla) caused by the presence of serum, or occasionally by an injected substance.

Bung - a cap or screw used to cover the small opening in the top of a metal drum or barrel.

Bunker Gear-Another name for Structural Firefighter Clothing

Burn - Refers to either a chemical or thermal burn, the former may be caused by corrosive substances and the latter by liquefied cryogenic gases, hot molten substances, or flames.

BW - Biological Weapons

BWC - Biological and Toxin Weapons Convention

BZ- Quinuclidinyl Benzilate (incapacitating agent)

C

C/B - Chemical/Biological

C3 - Command, Control, and Communications

CA is a highly irritating agent similar to CN. It is much more toxic that CN and is not used routinely any more. **alpha-bromophenylacetonitrile.** It is also called bromobenzylcyanide. It has been replaced by CN and CS

Cache - A pre-determined complement of tools, equipment, and/or supplies stored in a designated location, available for incident use.

CAER—Community Awareness and Emergency Response Voluntary programs aimed at providing support and coordination of public emergency response agencies, local government officials and facilities and businesses that use, store, handle, produce or transport hazardous materials

Calcification - process by which organic tissue becomes hardened by a deposit of calcium salts within its' substance

Calibrate – The process of determining the relative response of equipment or instruments and comparing the results to a known quantity or standard.

CAM - Chemical Agent Monitor

CAMEO - Acronym for Computer Aided Management of Emergency Operations A set of Software developed by the National Oceanic and Atmospheric Administration to aid in managing an incident. CAMEO includes a chemical database of the most common chemicals encountered by Emergency Responders.

Camp - A geographical site, within the general incident area, separate from the Incident Base, equipped and staffed to provide sleeping, food, water, and sanitary services to incident personnel.

CANA - Convulsive Antidote, Nerve Agent

Carbamates - A class of insecticides with similar chemical structure. Heavily used insecticides such as Baygon® , Sevin® and Ficam® all are carbamates.

Carboy - a bottle or rectangular container for liquids of about 5-to 15-gallon capacity that is made of glass, plastic, or metal and is often cushioned in a protective container.

Carbuncle - Deep-seated pyogenic infection of the skin and subcutaneous tissues, usually arising in several contiguous hair follicles, with formation of connecting sinuses; often preceded or accompanied by fever, malaise, and prostration.

CARC - Chemical Agent Resistant Coating

Carcinogen - Material capable of producing cancer. A chemical substance known to induce neoplastic change (malignancies) in experimental animals and/or man. Four types of response are generally accepted as evidence of induction of neoplasms:

  a. An increase in incidence of the tumor types that occur in controls.
  b. The development of tumors earlier than controls.
  c. The occurrence of tumor types not observed in controls.
  d. An increased multiplicity of tumors.

Carcinogenic - The cancer producing property of a substance or agent, producing or inciting cancer.

Carcinogenicity - The potential for development of cancer in a living individual. A cancer is a malignant tumor resulting from a change in the normal growth and development of cells. (Cancerous tumors have the tendency to invade surrounding tissue and spread to other sites in the body.)

Cardiac - pertaining to the heart

Cargo Manifest - a shipping paper that contains all of the contents being carried by the transporting vehicle or vessel.

Carrier - An inert liquid, solid, or gas added to an active ingredient to make a pesticide dispense effectively. A carrier is also the material, usually water or oil, used to dilute the formulated product for application.

CAS Identification Number - Chemical Abstracts Service. A number assigned to each unique chemical entity by the Chemical Abstract Service of the American Chemical Society. The CAS # provides information about the nature of the material and is unique for each registered compound.

Catalyst - A substance which, when present in a very small amount, increases the rate at which two or more chemicals react together, without being changed itself by the reaction.

Cathartic - causing evacuation of the bowels; laxative

Caustic - A substance that attacks tissue by chemical action. A corrosive substance is one that will destroy or irreversibly damage another substance with which it comes into contact. Caustics are traditionally considered basic materials because of the names like **caustic soda** (sodium hydroxide) and caustic **potash** (potassium hydroxide).

Caution - A term used on a precautionary label to denote a lowest degree of chemical hazard. A "Signal Word" used in the GHS Safety Data Sheet and Labeling Program.

CB - Chemical/Biological

CBDCOM - Chemical and Biological Defense Command

CBIRF – Chemical Biological Incident Response Force

CBPS - Chemical and Biological Protective Shelter

CBRNE – Chemical, Biological, Radiological, Nuclear and Energetic materials

CC - Usually means closed cup flash point.

cc - Cubic centimeter. A metric-system volume measurement equal to a milliliter (ml). One quart is about 946 cc (946 ml).

CDC - Centers for Disease Control and Prevention

CDC - Chemical Decontamination Center (Military)

Ceiling level (TLV-C) - Maximum concentration of toxic substance that cannot be exceeded even momentarily. Serious harm could occur if exposed above ceiling level concentration.

Ceiling Limit - The maximum allowable exposure limit for an airborne chemical, which is not to be exceeded even momentarily.

Ceiling Value - Normally refers to the maximum allowable exposure concentration at any time, for any duration. Practically, it may be an average value over the minimum time required to detect and measure the specified concentration.

Center Pin - The large steel pin which passes through the center of both the body and truck center plates and assists in keeping the two plates in proper alignment.

Center Sill - The main longitudinal structural member in a car underframe often constructed as a large box section. The center sill receives all of the buff and draft forces created in train handling and switching.

Centigrade - A measure of temperature. Water Freezes at 0°C and Boils at 100°C

Central Nervous System - The part of the body made up of the brain, spinal cord, and nerves.

Central Nervous System Depressants - Toxicants that deaden the central nervous system (CNS), diminishing sensation.

CERCLA - The Comprehensive Environmental Response, Compensation, and Liability Act of 1980—the Federal statute that authorized "Superfund." Administered by EPA, the law provides funding for cleanups and emergency response actions for hazardous substances at the worst hazardous waste sites in the United States. CERCLA is also significant because it set the first criteria for notification of emergencies involving hazardous substances. Superfund regulates abandoned waste disposal sites; for active disposal site regulation, see RCRA.

Certified Applicators - Individuals who are certified to use or supervise the use of any restricted use pesticide covered by their certification.

Chain of Command - A series of command, control, executive, or management positions in hierarchical order of authority.

Check-In - The process through which resources first report to an incident. Check-in locations include the incident command post, Resources Unit, incident base, camps, staging areas, or directly on the site.

Chemical Agent - A chemical substance intended for use in military operations to kill, seriously injure, or incapacitate people through its physiological effects.

Included are blood, nerve, choking, blister, and incapacitating agents. Excluded are riot control agents, chemical herbicides and smoke and flame materials.

Chemical Asphyxiant - Referred to as blood poisons, these are compounds that interrupt the flow of oxygen in the blood or the tissues in three ways:
  (1) They react more readily than oxygen with the blood. Carbon monoxide is the best-known example.
  (2) They liberate the hemoglobin from red blood cells, resulting in a lack of transport for oxygen. Hydrazine is one such asphyxiant.
  (3) They cause a malfunction in the oxygen-carrying ability of the red blood cells. Benzene and toluene are two of these.

Chemical Change – The process of changing the chemical structure of a material. Bonds are broken and new bonds are formed between different atoms.

Chemical Contamination - The presence of a chemical agent on a person, object, or area.

Contamination density of a chemical agent is usually expressed either in milligrams or grams per square meter (mg/m2, g/m2) or in pounds per hectare (lb/ha). Hectare is 10,000 square meters.

Chemical Control - Pesticide application to kill pests.

Chemosterilant - A chemical compound capable of preventing animal reproduction.

Chemical family - A group of single elements or compounds with a common structural feature, For example, acetone, methyl ethyl ketone (MEK), and methyl isobutyl ketone (MIBK) are members of the ketone family. Members of the family have the same chemical properties, but different physical properties.

Chemical formula - Gives the number and kind of atoms that make up a molecule. The chemical formula for water is H2O. Water is made up of 2 atoms of hydrogen and 1 atom of oxygen.

Chemical Name – In a Safety Data Sheet, the scientific name of the active ingredient(s) found in the formulated product. This complex name is derived from the chemical structure of the active ingredient.

Chemical properties - Description of how the chemical reacts to different chemicals or outside sources of energy.

Chemical Protective Clothing - Items such as clothing, hood, boots and gloves made from chemical-resistant materials that are designed and configured to protect the wearer from hazardous materials.

Chemical Reactivity - Reactivity refers to the rate at which a chemical substance tends to undergo a chemical reaction in time. In pure compounds, reactivity is regulated by the physical properties of the sample. For instance, grinding a sample to a higher specific surface area increases its reactivity

CHEMTREC - The CHEMical TRansportation Emergency Center, a public service of the Chemical Manufacturers Association. Located in Washington D.C. Available 24 hours a day. (1- 800-424-9300). Provides information and other assistance to emergency responders.

Cheyne-Stokes respiration - respiratory distress related to posture (especially reclining at night) that occurs in association with heart disease

Chief - The ICS title for individuals responsible for management of functional sections - Operations, Planning, Logistics, Finance/Administration, and Intelligence (if established as a separate section).

Class I Railroad - A railroad whose operating revenues are more than an annually designated amount- $ 255 million (1998 definition).

Class II Railroad - A railroad whose operating revenues are between $ 20.4 million and the Class I threshold.

Classification Yard – A rail yard consisting of any number of usually parallel tracks, used for sorting railcars by destination and making up trains. Also referred to as a "call yard". These facilities may have locomotive and car repair and servicing facilities, fueling operations and other railroad support activities.

Chloracne - acne-like eruption caused by exposure to chlorine compounds

Chlorinated – Containing one or more chlorine atoms. Especially--A group of insecticides which contains carbon, hydrocarbons, hydrogen and chlorine. Chlordane, Aldrin, Heptachlor and Lindane are all examples of Chlorinated

Hydrocarbons.

Choking Agent - A pulmonary agent (or choking agent) is a chemical weapon agent designed to impede a victim's ability to breathe. They operate by causing a build-up of fluids in the lungs which then leads to suffocation (pulmonary edema). Death results from lack of oxygen; hence, the victim is "choked." Common examples are chlorine and phosgene.

Cholera - A diarrheal disease caused by Vibrio cholera, a short, curved, gram-negative bacillus. Humans acquire the disease by consuming water or food contaminated with the organism. The organism multiplies in the small intestine and secretes an enterotoxin that causes a secretory diarrhea. If used as a biological warfare agent, it would most likely be used to contaminate water supplies.

Cholinesterase - A body enzyme needed for the proper operation of the nervous system. Nerve Agents such as Soman and many organophosphorus insecticides are cholinesterase inhibitors.

CHRIS - An acronym for the Chemical Hazard Response Information System. Written and maintained by the United States Coast Guard.

Chronic - persistent or prolonged injury. Of long duration or having frequent recurrence or exposure.

Chronic Effects - Long-lasting results of exposure to a toxin; can be a permanent change caused by a single, acute exposure or a continuous, low-level exposure. Chronic health effects are those that become apparent or continue for some time after exposure to a hazardous material.

Chronic Exposure - Continuous or repeated exposure to a substance over a long period of time, typically the greater part of the total life-span in animals or plants (usually, several years in humans).

Ciliary - Pertaining to certain structures in the eye, such as the ciliary muscles.

CINC - Commander in Chief

Ciprofloxacin - An antibiotic drug useful in treating bacterial infections; the recommended antibiotic for treating anthrax infections as well as prophylaxis in a biological warfare setting. Sometimes referred to as only "Cipro"

cis - refers to a specific arrangement of atoms within a chemical molecule.

CJCS - Chairman of the Joint Chiefs of Staff

Clear Text - The use of plain English in radio communications transmissions. No Ten Codes or agency-specific codes are used when utilizing clear text.

Clonic - pertaining to alternate muscular contraction and relaxation in rapid succession

Clostridium Perfringens Toxins - A common anaerobic bacterium associated with three distinct disease syndromes: gas gangrene or clostridial myonecrosis, enteritis necroticans, and clostridium food poisoning.

CMA - Chemical Manufacturers Association.

CN- Chloroacetophenone CN (1-chloroacetophenone) is the standard tear gas used by law enforcement agencies

CNS - Central Nervous System.

COCOM - Coordinating Committee for Multilateral Export Controls

COD - Chemical Oxygen Demand - A means of measuring the pollution impact of organic chemicals in water.

COFC - Container on flat car—Railroad shipment where the container—typically an intermodal chemical container—is placed on a flat car.

Cold zone - Area where the command post and support functions that are necessary to control an incident are located. This is also referred to as the clean zone or support zone in other documents.

Cold Work - deformation of steel when it is bent at ambient temperatures or as a result of an impact. Cold work can sharply increase the transition temperature where the cold work has taken place and reduce the ductility of the steel.

Combustible - Can catch fire and burn.

Combustible liquid - Liquids which have a flash point greater than 60.5°C (141°F) and below 93°C (200°F). U.S. regulations permit a flammable liquid flashing between 38°C (100°F) and 60.5°C (141°F) to be reclassed as a combustible liquid.

Combustion - The process of burning.

Command - The act of directing, ordering, or controlling by virtue of explicit statutory, regulatory, or delegated authority.

Command Post - A centralized base of operations established near the site of a hazardous materials incident.

Command Staff - In an incident management organization, the Command Staff consists of the Incident Command and the special staff positions of Public Information Officer, Safety Officer, Liaison Officer, and other positions as required, who report directly to the Incident Commander. They may have an assistant or assistants, as needed.

Command - The act of directing and/or controlling resources by virtue of explicit legal, agency, or delegated authority. May also refer to the Incident Commander.

Commodity – A general term used to describe the contents of a car. Other terms such as "lading", "product" or "grade" mean the same thing and are often used interchangeably.

Commodity stencil - The proper name stenciled on the side of the rail car describing the lading or product the car is designed or constructed to hold, generally in a dedicated service basis. (i.e., sulfuric acid, liquefied petroleum gas, chlorine.) See 49 CFR for list of hazardous materials required to be stenciled on tank cars.

Common Operating Picture - A broad view of the overall situation as reflected by situation reports, aerial photography, and other information or intelligence.

Communication Unit - An Organizational Unit in the Logistics Section responsible for providing communication services at an incident. A Communication Unit may also be a facility (e.g., a trailer or mobile van) used to provide the major part of an Incident Communications Center..

Compacts - Formal working agreements among agencies to obtain mutual aid.

Compatible - When two different products can be mixed without affecting the properties of either one.

Compensation/Claims Unit - Functional Unit within the Finance/Administration Section responsible for financial concerns resulting from property damage, injuries, or fatalities at the incident.

Complex - Two or more individual incidents located in the same general area that are assigned to a single Incident Commander or to Unified Command.

Compound - A substance formed by two or more elements or ingredients in definite proportion by weight.

Compressed Gas - any material or mixture having in the container absolute pressure exceeding 40 pounds per square inch gauge (psig) at 70°F, or having an absolute pressure exceeding 104 psig at 130°F.

Compressed Gas in Solution - a non-liquified gas that is dissolved at high pressure in a solvent. For example, most acetylene used for welding is acetylene gas dissolved in a solvent inside a pressurized cylinder.

Concentration - A term used to indicate the amount of an active ingredient that is contained in a given mixture-solid, liquid or gas. The amount of one substance mixed or dissolved in a specified amount of a second substance. The amount of a product measured by a certain volume or weight of that material in another material.

Condensation - The conversion of a vapor into a liquid as it is cooled down to or below the liquid's boiling point.

Confined Space - A space that has limited openings for entry and exit and has poor natural ventilation.

Confinement - Actions taken to keep a material in a defined or local area after it is released.

Conjunctiva - The delicate membrane that lines the eyelids and covers the exposed surface of the sclera.

Conjunctival - Pertaining to conjunctiva.

Conjunctivitis - inflammation of the lining of the eyelids

Consignee - the person who is to receive the shipment.

Consist - a rail shipping paper similar to a cargo manifest. It may contain a list of cars in the train in order or a list of those cars containing hazardous materials and their location on the train.

Contagious - Of a disease, easily transmitted to others

Container - an article of transport equipment which is (a) of a permanent character and strong enough for repeated use; (b) specifically designed to facilitate the carriage of goods by one or more modes of transport without intermediate reloading; and (c) fitted with devices permitting its transfer from one mode to another.

Container Chassis - a trailer chassis having simply a frame with locking devices for securing and transporting a container as a wheeled vehicle.

Container Ship - a ship specially equipped to transport large freight containers in horizontal or more commonly, in vertical container cells. The containers are loaded and unloaded usually by special cranes.

Containment - those procedures taken to keep a material in its container.

Contaminated - Containing potentially harmful material.

Contamination - A release of hazardous material from its source to people, animals, the environment or equipment. The presence of hazardous substances in the environment. From the public health perspective, environmental contamination is addressed when it potentially affects the health and quality of life of people living and working near contamination.

Contamination is the presence of a minor constituent in another chemical or mixture, often at the trace level. In chemistry, the term usually describes a single chemical, but in specialized fields the term can also mean chemical mixtures, even up to the level of cellular materials.

Contamination is the deposit of radioactive material on the surface of structures, areas, objects, or personnel, following a nuclear explosion. This material generally consists of weapon debris becoming incorporated with particles of dirt, etc. Contamination can also arise from radioactivity induced in certain substances by the action of neutrons from a nuclear explosion.

Contraindication - any condition which renders some particular line of treatment improper or undesirable

Control - the procedures, techniques, and methods used in the mitigation of a hazardous materials incident, including containment, extinguishment, and confinement. Broken down into Offensive, Defensive, and nonintervention.

Control zones – The areas at hazardous materials incidents that are designated based upon the degree of hazard. These areas are defined as HOT, WARM, or COLD.

Controlled Burn - Defensive or nonintervention tactical objective by which a fire is allowed to burn with no effort to extinguish it.

Convection - The transfer of heat through a liquid or gas by the actual movement of the molecules.

Convulsion - An abnormal violent and involuntary contraction or series of contractions of the voluntary muscles.

Convulsant - a drug which induces convulsions and/or epileptic seizures, the opposite of an anticonvulsant. These drugs generally act as stimulants at low doses, but are not used for this purpose due to the risk of convulsions and consequent excitotoxicity.

Cooperating Agency - An agency supplying assistance other than direct operational or support functions or resources to the incident management effort.

Coordinate - To advance systematically an analysis and exchange of information among principals who have or may have a need to know certain information to carry out specific incident management responsibilities.

Coordination Center - A facility that is used for the coordination of agency or jurisdictional resources in support of one or more incidents.

Coordination - The process of systematically analyzing a situation, developing relevant information, and informing appropriate command authority of viable alternatives for selection of the most effective combination of available resources to meet specific objectives. The coordination process (which can be either intra- or interagency) does not involve dispatch actions. However, personnel responsible for coordination may perform command or dispatch functions within the limits established by specific agency delegations, procedures, legal authority, etc.

Corium - The deeper layer of the skin under the epidermis. It contains the hair follicles, sweat glands, and sebaceous glands.

Cornea, corneal - The clear, transparent, anterior portion of the eye comprising about one-sixth of its surface through which light passes to transmit images to the retina. It is continuous at its periphery with the schlera and composed of five layers.

Corner Fittings - strong metal devices, located at the corners of an intermodal container, having several apertures which normally provide the means for handling, stacking, and securing the freight container.

Corner Structures - vertical frame components located at the corners of an intermodal container, integral with the corner fittings.

Corrective Actions - actions taken by the incident commander to correct the problem at hand in a hazardous materials emergency.

Corrosive - Any material which causes visible damage or irreversible alteration of human tissue (skin, eyes, etc.) at the site of contact or causes metals or plastics to corrode at a rapid rate.

Corrosivity - A measure or tendency of a substance to cause deterioration in another material.

Covalent Compound – A material with a covalent bond. A covalent bond is a form of chemical bonding that is characterized by the sharing of pairs of electrons between atoms, and other covalent bonds.

Cost Sharing Agreements - Agreements between agencies or jurisdictions to share designated costs related to incidents. Cost sharing agreements are normally written but may also be oral between authorized agency or jurisdictional representatives at the incident.

Cost Unit - Functional Unit within the Finance/Administration Section responsible for tracking costs, analyzing cost data, making cost estimates, and recommending cost-saving measures.

CPC- Chemical Protective Clothing.

CPC - Counter Proliferation Council

CPR - Acronym for Cardiopulmonary Resuscitation an emergency procedure used to maintain and restore breathing and blood circulation.

CPRC - Counter Proliferation Program Review Committee

CPS - Chemical Protective Shelter

Crack & Crevice Treatment - Application of small quantities of pesticides into cracks and crevices with no residual on outside surfaces.

Crew - See Single Resource.

Crimean-Congo Hemorrhagic Fever - A viral disease caused by Crimean-Congo Hemorrhagic Fever virus. The virus is transmitted by ticks, principally of the genus Hyalomma. Humans become infected through tick bites, crushing an infected tick, or at the slaughter of viremic livestock. If used as a biological warfare agent, it would most likely be delivered by aerosol.

Critical pressure - The minimum pressure above which a gas cannot be liquefied no matter what the temperature is.

Critical temperature - The minimum temperature above which a gas cannot be liquefied no matter how much pressure is applied.

Crop - Any plant which is growing where it is wanted.

Crossover Line - installed in tank piping system to allow unloading from either side of tank

Cryogenic - Extremely cold. Danger of frostbite, instantaneous freezing of tissue, freezing of PPE, embrittlement of other materials. Usually considered to be a liquid with a boiling point less than - 130°F. Pertaining to or causing the production of low temperatures

Cryogenic liquid - A refrigerated, liquefied gas that has a boiling point colder than -90°C (-130°F) at atmospheric pressure.

Cryogenic Tank Car - A tank car used to transport refrigerated liquids at low pressure, usually 25 psig or lower at temperatures of -130°F and lower. Cryogenic tank cars are typically a tank-within-a-tank style with an inner space filled with insulation and or a vacuum.

CS - US military designator for a variant of tear gas with chemical name O-chlorobenzylidene malononitrile. This is the standard military tear gas. It is about 10 times as strong as CN.

Ct - This means concentration times time. Note that a 2-minute exposure to a concentration of 100 mg/m3 [Ct = 200 mg min/m3 (milligram-minutes per cubic meter)], does NOT necessarily produce the same toxicological effects as a 50-minute exposure to a concentration of 4 mg/m3 (Ct = 200 mg min/m3).

Ct Value - A measure of vapor or gas exposure by inhalation. It is a product of the concentration usually expressed in mg/m3 and duration of exposure (t) in minutes. The resulting (and somewhat confusing units) are mg min/m3. It is important to recognize that this is not simple algebra; predictions of toxic effects should never be extrapolated more than twice, or less than half, known toxic exposure data. (Exposure to 1 mg/m3 for 20 minutes; 2 mg/m3 for 10 minutes; or 4 mg/m3 for 5 minutes are all valid extrapolations of 2-minute exposure data. All three equate to a Ct of 20 mg min/m3.)

CTBT - Comprehensive Test Ban Treaty

CTR - Cooperative Threat Reduction

CTTS - Counterterror Technical Support

CVS - Cardiovascular system.

Curie (Ci) - An older unit of radioactive decay rate defined as 3.7×10^{10} disintegrations per second. The gamma curie is sometimes defined correspondingly as the activity of material in which this number of gamma-ray photons are emitted per second.

CW - Chemical Weapons

CWC - Chemical Weapons Convention

CWD - Chemical Weapons Destruction

Cyanosis, cyanotic - A dark bluish / purplish coloration of the skin, mucous membranes, lips, or fingernails caused by lack of oxygen utilization by the body.

Cyclitis - Inflammation of the ciliary body of the eye.

Cyclohexyl sarin- a variant of sarin made with a cyclohexyl ring. This is a G-series nerve agent with chemical name O-Cyclohexyl-methylfluorophosphonate. NATO designator is GF.

Cyclonite or RDX also called hexogen, Research Department Explosive, and Royal Demolition Explosive. Used in Plastic Explosives for legitimate and terrorist purposes. Cyclotrimethylenetrinitramine.

Cytotoxin - Toxin that directly damages and kills the cell with which is makes contact.

CX US military designator for phosgene oxime. Although phosgene oxime is not a blister agent, it is treated as one by the military. Phosgene oxime is more correctly referred to as an urticant- an agent that causes painful welts on contact with skin.

D

Danger - A term used on a precautionary label to denote the highest degree of chemical hazard.

Dangerous Cargo Manifest - cargo manifest used on ships that contains a list of all the hazardous materials on board, including their location.

Dangerous goods - This term is used to describe articles or substances which are capable of posing a significant risk to health, safety, or to property when offered for transport and which are classified according to appropriate sections of the International Air Transport Association (IATA) regulations or the International Maritime Dangerous Goods (IMDG) regulations.

Dangerously Reactive Material - A material that can react by itself (e.g. polymerization) or with air or water to produce a hazardous condition.

DARPA - Defense Advanced Research Projects Agency

DBDO - Desert Battle Dress Over-garment

Deactivation - The process by which the toxic action of a pesticide is reduced or eliminated by impurities in the spray tank by water being used for mixing, or by biotic or abiotic factors in the environment.

Decay - The decrease in activity of any radioactive material with the passage of time due to spontaneous emission from the atomic nuclei of either alpha or beta particles, sometimes accompanied by gamma radiation.

Decoction - Mixture prepared by boiling components together

Decompose - Breaking apart into smaller different chemicals.

Decomposition - The breakdown of a material into simpler compounds by chemical reaction, decay, heat, or other process. May be violent.

Decomposition products - Products of a chemical or thermal break-down of a substance.

Decomposition Temperature- the temperature at which a material begins to decompose and change composition. This temperature may cause only minor effects (loss of product quality, etc.) or it may be destructive liberating heat or more toxic materials.

Decontaminate - To remove or neutralize a material so it or the environment it is in are safe.

Decontamination - The removal and/or neutralization of chemical, biological or radiological contamination from personnel, equipment, or other material. This process is critical to health and safety at hazardous waste incidents.

Decontamination Area - Area located on the upwind edge of the Hot Zone used to decontaminate personnel and equipment. All personnel coming out of the Hot Zone must pass through the Decontamination Area for decontamination.

Decontamination Corridor- The area established to do decontamination typically containing several "Stations" to clean the person, equipment, etc. In theory each Station of the Decontamination Corridor should remove substantial contaminant so that at the end of the corridor the person or equipment is no longer contaminated above levels of concern.

Deflagration - an explosion characterized by rapid combustion rather than a detonation. The burning which takes place at a speed below the velocity of sound. The difference between Deflagration and Detonation is the speed of burning.

Degradation - a type of decomposition characteristic of high molecular weight substances such as proteins, polymers, branched-chained sulfonates etc. It may result from oxidation, heat, sunlight, solvents, material action, or in the case of body proteins from infectious microorganisms. A concern when selecting PPE is the degradation of the chemical suit materials to the point where they are no longer protective

Dehydrating - Chemical or physical removal of water from a substance.

Delayed - toxic effect occurring after a lapse of time

Delegation of Authority - A statement provided to the Incident Commander by the Agency Executive delegating authority and assigning responsibility. The Delegation of Authority can include objectives, priorities, expectations, constraints, and other considerations or guidelines as needed. Many agencies require written Delegation of Authority to be given to Incident Commanders prior to their assuming command on larger incidents.

Deliquescent - Material absorbs water from the air becoming liquid.

Deluge - A flooding quantity of water.

Deluge System- A firefighting or fire-suppression system causing the spray or release of large quantities of water

Demobilization Unit - Functional Unit within the Planning Section responsible for assuring orderly, safe, and efficient demobilization of incident resources.

Demulcent – soothing

Dengue - An acute infectious disease caused by an arbovirus transmitted by **Aedes aegypti** mosquitoes characterized by fever, chills, headache, nausea, vomiting, rash, and severe muscle and joint pains.

Density - Measure of how heavy a unit volume of a substance is. Often expressed in lbs/gal (pounds per gallon), g/cc (grams per cubic centimeter) or lbs/ft3 (pounds per cubic foot).

Dents - A deformation of the tank shell or head caused by contact with a blunt object.

Deposition – The process of going directly from a vapor state to a solid state without passing through the liquid state.

Deputy - A fully qualified individual who, in the absence of a superior, can be delegated the authority to manage a functional operation or perform a specific task. In some cases, a deputy can act as relief for a superior and, therefore, must be fully qualified in the position. Deputies can be assigned to the Incident Commander, General Staff, and Branch Directors.

Derail - A safety device, attached to one rail of a siding, storage, or repair track, that will cause a railcar to be derailed in the event it rolls free towards a main track or work area where it could cause a major accident. May be a single directional or a bi-directional device.

Dermal - Pertaining to the skin. One of the major ways pesticides can enter the body to possibly cause poisoning.

Dermal Exposure - Exposure to toxic substances by entry though the skin.

Dermatitis - An inflammation or infection of the skin.

Desiccant - Chemical used to accelerate drying (removal of water). A pesticide that destroys target pests by causing them to lose body moisture. A drying agent

DET Cord—Detonation Cord—Used to set off explosive devices or multiple explosives in earth moving operations.

Detection Limit - Analytical capability based on the amount of the sample and the sensitivity of the analytical method.

Detonate - The rapid decomposition of an explosive material leading to a rapidly moving wave of high temperature and high pressure. May be started by impact, friction or heat.

Detonation - a wave that passes along the body of an explosive, instantaneously converting the explosive into gas.

DF The military designator for a precursor combined with isopropyl alcohol to form GB (Sarin) as a binary weapon.

DGP - NATO Senior Defense Group on Proliferation

DIA - Defense Intelligence Agency

Diffusion - The process of spontaneous intermixing of different substances due to molecular motion which tends to produce uniformity of concentration.

Dike - temporary walls constructed to halt the flow of a liquid substance; earthen or concrete walls surrounding oil tanks designed to catch overflow from tanks and relieve the danger of flowing flammable liquids spreading to other exposures.

Diluent - a diluting agent

Dilution - Increase the volume of solvent, which decreases the amount of solute (material that is dissolved). For example, diluting an acid with water reduces the strength of the acid and its hazardous properties.

Director - The ICS title for individuals responsible for supervision of a Branch.

Dirty Bomb—An explosive device containing radioactive materials. The purpose of "Dirty Bombs" is to contaminate a large area with radioactivity.

Dispatch - The ordered movement of a resource or resources to an assigned operational mission or an administrative move from one location to another.

Dispatch Center - A facility from which resources are ordered, mobilized, and assigned to an incident.

Dispatch - The implementation of a command decision to move a resource or resources from one place to another.

Disperse - To scatter in different directions.

Dissociation – The amount of ionization by an acid or base. Measured on a logarithmic scale. See pKa.

Diuresis - increased secretion of urine

Diuretic - agent that increases urine production

Division - The partition of an incident into geographical areas of operation. Divisions are established when the number of resources exceeds the manageable span of control of the Operations Chief. A division is located within the ICS organization between the branch and resources in the Operations Section. Division - Divisions are used to divide an incident into geographical areas of operation. A Division is located within the ICS organization between the Branch and the Task Force/Strike Team. (See Group.) Divisions are identified by alphabetic characters for horizontal applications and, often, by floor numbers when used in buildings.

DMZ - Demilitarized Zone

DOC - Department Operations Center

Documentation Unit - Functional Unit within the Planning Section responsible for collecting, recording, and safeguarding all documents relevant to the incident.

DoD - Department of Defense

DOE - Department of Energy

Dose - Toxicologists generally define the dose as the amount of material applied to the organism. The amount actually absorbed into the body is referred to as the internal or systemic dose. The quantity of a chemical that is absorbed in the body and is available for interaction with metabolic processes. A (total or accumulated) quantity of radiation. The absorbed dose in rads represents the amount of energy absorbed from radiation per gram of specified absorbed material.

Dose Response - describes the change in effect on an organism caused by differing levels of exposure (or doses) to a stressor (usually a chemical) after a certain exposure time.

Dose-Response Relationship - The relationship between (1) the dose, often based on an "administered dose" (i.e., exposure) rather than absorbed dose, and (2) the extent of toxic injury produced by that chemical. The response can increase with greater doses and can be expressed either as the severity of injury or proportion of exposed subjects affected.

Dosage - The measured quantity of a product used at one time.

DOT - Department of Transportation

Dry chemical - A preparation designed for fighting fires involving flammable liquids, pyrophoric substances and electrical equipment. Common types contain sodium bicarbonate or potassium bicarbonate.

Dry Flowable - A dry, granular pesticide formulation intended to be mixed with water for application. When combined with water, a dry flowable will be similar to a wettable powder. Dry flowable formulations are measure by volume rather than weight.

DS2 - standard decontaminant for chemical warfare agents; contains 70% diethylene triamine, 28% ethylene glycol monomethyl ether, and 2% sodium hydroxide. Note that DS2 is corrosive to skin and may cause serious burns to exposed flesh.

DSWA - Defense Special Weapons Agency

DTD - Detailed Troop Decontamination

DTSA - Defense Technology Security Administration

Ductile - a property of metals--capable of being drawn out or hammered thin

Dust - Airborne solid particles much larger than aerosols.

Dust - Finely ground pesticide particles, sometimes combined with inert materials. Dusts are applied without mixing with water or other liquid.

Dyspnea - Labored breathing resulting from an increased need for oxygen or inadequate air exchange in the lungs.

E

Eastern Equine Encephalitis - A member of the Alphavirus family transmitted by mosquitos that generally infect horses but can cause epidemics in humans. Those infected present symptoms of malaise, headache, nausea, and vomiting.

Ebola - An RNA virus of the Filovirus family that causes one of the viral hemorrhagic fevers. Contact with infected body fluids rather than aerosols may be the principal mode of transmission. The incubation period is 20 to 21 days. The initial symptoms are fever, headache, sore throat, abdominal pain, vomiting and diarrhea. Those patients who exhibit hemorrhage usually follow a downhill course to shock and death.

Economically Important Pest - An insect or plant whose presence can damage crops or property in a measurable value.

ECP - Entry Control Point

ECt50 - The dosage causing a specifically defined effect in 50 percent of the given population. The route of exposure can be either inhalation or percutaneous (PC). Similarly, the **ECt05, ECt16, ECt84,** and **ECt95** are the dosages causing that defined effect in 5 percent, 16 percent, 84percent, and 95 percent of the given population, respectively.

Ectoparasiticide - an agent that kills parasites living on the exterior of its host

ED50 - The dosage of liquid agent causing a specifically defined effect in 50 percent of the given population. Within this context, ED50 refers to a percutaneous liquid exposure. Unless otherwise specified, all ED50s are for percutaneous liquid contamination of bare skin. Similarly, the **ED05, ED16, ED84,** and **ED95** are the dosages causing that defined effect in 5 percent, 16 percent, 84 percent, and 95 percent of the given population, respectively.

ED50 (Median Effective Dose) - The dose of a substance that produces a given, defined therapeutic or toxic effect in 50 percent of the exposed population. NOT A 50 PERCENT EFFECT! This is a quantal (yes/no) determination, but it can be applied to graded effects if they are defined in a quantal manner (e.g., the dose of drug necessary to decrease diastolic blood pressure by 10 millimeters (mm) mercury (Hg) in 50 percent of the subjects). Under these circumstances, it is imperative that the assumptions and definition of "effect" be stated with the dose.

Edema - presence of abnormally large amounts of fluid in intercellular spaces of body tissues. Swelling of the tissues because of fluid.

Edema - The accumulation of an excessive amount of watery fluid in cells and tissues. Pulmonary edema is an excessive buildup of water in the lungs, for instance, after inhalation of a gas that is corrosive to lung tissue.

Edible - A food; safe to eat.

EDMIN - The dose that will predictably cause minimal effects in 50% of those exposed.

EDS - Equipment Decontamination Station

Efficacy - The effectiveness of a product; its inherent ability to do what it says it will do.

EGDN—Ethylene Glycol DiNitrate—an explosive material similar in properties to Nitroglycerin used in dynamites designed for colder climates.

Electromagnetic Radiation - A traveling wave motion resulting from oscillating magnetic and electric fields. Familiar electromagnetic radiations range from X rays, through the ultraviolet, visible, and infrared regions, to radar and radio waves. All electromagnetic radiations travel, in a vacuum, with the velocity of light.

Electron - A particle of very small mass, carrying a unit negative charge. Electrons, surrounding the nucleus, are present in all atoms; their number is equal to the number of positive charges (or protons) in the particular nucleus.

Element - One of the distinct, basic varieties of matter occurring in nature which, individually or in combination, compose substances of all kinds. There are 91 different elements known to exist in nature and others, including plutonium, have been obtained as a result of nuclear reactions.

EMAC - Emergency Management Assistance Compact

Emergency - Absent a Presidentially declared emergency, any incident(s), human-caused or natural, that requires responsive action to protect life or property. Under the Robert T. Stafford Disaster Relief and Emergency Assistance Act, an emergency means any occasion or instance for which, in the determination of the President, Federal assistance is needed to supplement State and local efforts and capabilities to save lives and to protect property and public health and safety, or to lessen or avert the threat of a catastrophe in any part of the United States.

Emergency Management Coordinator/Director - The individual within each political subdivision that has coordination responsibility for jurisdictional emergency management.

Emergency Operations Centers (EOCs) - The physical location at which the coordination of information and resources to support domestic incident management activities normally takes place. An EOC may be a temporary facility or may be located in a more central or permanently established facility, perhaps at a higher level of organization within a jurisdiction. EOCs may be organized by major functional disciplines (e.g., fire, law enforcement, and medical services), by jurisdiction (e.g., Federal, State, regional, county, city, tribal), or some combination thereof.

Emergency Operations Centers (EOCs) - The physical location at which the coordination of information and resources to support domestic incident management activities normally takes place. An EOC may be a temporary facility or may be located in a more central or permanently established facility, perhaps at a higher level of organization within a jurisdiction. EOCs may be organized by major functional disciplines (e.g., fire, law enforcement, and medical services), by jurisdiction (e.g., Federal, State, regional, county, city, tribal), or some combination thereof.

Emergency Operations Plan - The "steady-state" plan maintained by various jurisdictional levels for responding to a wide variety of potential hazards.

Emergency Operations Plan (EOP) - The plan that each jurisdiction has and maintains for responding to appropriate hazards.

Emergency Public Information - Information that is disseminated primarily in anticipation of an emergency or during an emergency. In addition to providing situational information to the public, it also frequently provides directive actions required to be taken by the general public.

Emergency Response Provider - Includes Federal, State, local, and tribal emergency public safety, law enforcement, emergency response, emergency medical (including hospital emergency facilities), and related personnel, agencies, and Act of 2002, Pub. L. 107-296, 116 Stat. 2135 (2002). Also known as **Emergency Responder**.

Emesis - vomiting

Emphysema - Process of trapping air in the alveoli, associated with loss of elasticity of the lung tissues and resulting in inability to completely exhale.

Emulsifier - An adjuvant added to a pesticide formulation to permit petroleum-based pesticides to mix with water.

Emulsion - Mixture in which tiny droplets of one liquid (or solid) are suspended (trapped) in another liquid.

Encapsulation - A process by which tiny liquid droplets or dry particles are contained in polymer plastic capsules to slow their release into the environment and prolong their effectiveness. Sometimes encapsulation lowers hazards to people mixing or applying pesticides.

Endothermic - A process or chemical reaction that absorbs heat.

Enteritis - inflammation of the intestine

EOC - Emergency Operations Center

EOP - Emergency Operations Plan

EPA - Environmental Protection Agency

EPA Number - The number assigned to chemicals regulated by the United States Environmental Protection Agency (EPA).

EPCI - Enhanced Proliferation Control Initiative

Epidemiology - The branch of medical science that deals with the incidence, distribution, and control of disease in a population.

Epidemiology Studies - Investigation of factors contributing to disease or toxic effects in the

Epigastric - pertaining to the upper-middle region of the abdomen

Epileptiform - occurring in severe or sudden spasms

Epithelium - cells covering the internal and external surfaces of the body

Epithelium - The outer layer of the skin.

Eradication - The pest management technique that uses physical or chemical barriers to prevent certain pests from getting into a defined area.

Erathma - The rupturing of capillaries.

ERPG-1: the maximum airborne concentration below which it is believed that nearly all individuals could be exposed for up to one hour without experiencing other than mild transient adverse health effects or perceiving a clearly defined objectionable odor. (nuisance level)

ERPG-2: the maximum airborne concentration below which it is believed that nearly all individuals could be exposed to for up to one hour without experiencing or developing irreversible or other serious health effects or symptoms that could impair their abilities to take protective action. (Exposure results in non-life threatening, irreversible health effects and individuals are able to take protective action. An evacuation criterion)

ERPG-3: The maximum airborne concentration below which it is believed that nearly all individuals could be exposed for up to 1 hour without experiencing or developing life threatening health effects. (Exposure can cause serious health effects and may be life-threatening. An injury criterion)

Erythema - Red area of skin caused by heat or cold injury, trauma, or inflammation. May be localized or generalized. Redness of the skin produced by congestion of the capillaries.

Erythema - A severe redness of the skin, as caused by chemical poisoning or sunburn.

Etiologic – Events created by uncontrolled exposures to living microorganisms.

Etiologic agents - Viable microorganisms or their toxins that cause or may cause human disease.

Evacuation - Organized, phased, and supervised withdrawal, dispersal, or removal of civilians from dangerous or potentially dangerous areas, and their reception and care in safe areas. evaluation of the incident to identify lessons learned; post-incident reporting; and development of initiatives to mitigate the effects of future incidents.

Evaporation - Transfer of liquid molecules into the vapor (gas) state.

Evaporation Rate - The rate at which a chemical changes into a vapor. A chemical that evaporates quickly can be a more dangerous fire or health hazard.

Event - A planned, nonemergency activity. ICS can be used as the management system for a wide range of events, e.g., parades, concerts, or sporting events.

Excess Flow Valve - a safety valve designed to shut off the flow of a liquid when the rate exceeds a set rate.

Exercise - A simulated emergency condition carried out for the purpose of testing and evaluating the readiness of a community or organization to handle a particular type of emergency.

Exothermic - A process or chemical reaction that gives off heat

Expansion Ratio - considered the amount of gas produced by the evaporation of one volume of liquid at a given temperature

Explode - The rapid expansion of a material or container with the release of energy, heat or pressure.

Explosion - the sudden release of energy, usually in the form of large volumes of gas which exert pressure on the surrounding medium. The explosions may be deflagrations or detonations.

Explosive - Any substance designed to produce an explosion (i.e. an extremely rapid release of gas and heat) or capable of producing an explosion by reacting with itself. Characterized by or relating to bursting forth with sudden violence or noise from internal energy; relating to a rapid reaction with production of noise, heat, and violent expansion of gases.

Explosive (Regulatory Definitions)

   ATF Any chemical compound, mixture, or device with the primary or common purpose being to function by explosion. The term includes, but is not limited to: dynamite, black powder, pellet powder, initiating explosives, detonators, safety fuses, electric matches, detonating cords, igniter cords, and igniters.

   NFPA The term "explosives" includes any material determined to be within the scope of Title 18, United States Code, Chapter 40, Importation, Manufacture, Distribution, and Storage of Explosive Materials, and also includes any material classified as explosive by the Hazardous Material Regulations of DOT.

Explosive (Technical Definition) Any material that is capable of undergoing a self-contained and self-sustained exothermic chemical reaction at a rate that is sufficient to produce substantial pressures on their surroundings, thus causing physical damage. Explosives fall into 2 classes, detonating and deflagrating.

Exposure - The amount of chemical that enters the body by some route for a specified frequency and duration. The contact of an organism with some product or device.

Exposure Assessment - A process that takes into account the chemical and physical properties of the substance, the effect the substance produces, the exposure frequency and duration, and the affected subject.

Exposure Routes - The major routes of exposure include ingestion, inhalation, and absorption through the skin.

Extremely Flammable - In this volume, defined as the equivalent of NFPA Flammability Hazard Class 4 and GHS Class 1.

Extremely Hazardous Substances - The Environmental Protection Agency (EPA) uses this term to refer to chemicals which must be reported to the appropriate authorities if released in amounts above the threshold reporting quantity. A list of Extremely Hazardous Substances is identified in Title III of the Superfund Amendments and Reauthorization Act (SARA) of 1986 found in 40 CFR Part 355.

F

Facilities Unit - Functional Unit within the Support Branch of the Logistics Section that provides fixed facilities for the incident. These facilities may include the Incident Base, feeding areas, sleeping areas, sanitary facilities, etc.

Fallout - The process of the descent to the earth's surface of particles contaminated with radioactive material from a radioactive cloud. The term is also applied in a collective sense to the contaminated particulate matter itself. The early (or local) fallout is defined, somewhat arbitrarily, as those particles which reach the earth within 24 hours after a nuclear explosion. The delayed (or worldwide) fallout consists of the smaller particles which ascend into the upper troposphere and stratosphere, to be carried by winds to all parts of the earth. The delayed fallout is brought to earth, mainly by rain and snow, over extended periods ranging from months to years.

Fasciculation - Localized contraction of muscle fibers, usually visible through the skin.

FBI - Federal Bureau of Investigation

FDA - Food and Drug Administration

FEC - An acronym for Facility Emergency Coordinator.

Federal - Of or pertaining to the Federal Government of the United States of America.

FEMA - An acronym for United States Federal Emergency Management Agency.

Fibrosis - Scar tissue; replacement by fibrous tissue.

Field Operations Guide - A pocket-size manual of instructions on the application of the Incident Command System.

FIFRA - Federal Insecticide, Fungicide and Rodenticide Act

Finance/Administration Section - The Section responsible for all incident costs and financial considerations. Includes the Time Unit, Procurement Unit, Compensation/Claims Unit, and Cost Unit.

Fire Fighting Gear - Turnout gear including footwear, trousers, a coat, gloves, a helmet, and respiratory protection. (NFPA 472)

Fire point - The lowest temperature at which a liquid produces sufficient vapor to flash near its surface and to continue to burn. Usually 10 to 30 $^{\circ}$C higher than the flash point.

First Responder - The individual who arrives first at the scene of a Hazmat incident with the responsibility to act.

Flaccid paralysis - Loss of muscle tone and capability to function; limp. Nerve agents cause this condition.

Flammable - capable of being easily ignited and supporting combustion

Flammable Gas - in order to be considered a flammable gas, a chemical must have an LFL of 13 percent or below, or a flammable range of 12 percent.

Flammable liquid –
> **DOT** Class 3: **Flammable** Liquids. A **flammable** liquid is a liquid having a flash point of not more than 60 °C (140 °F), or any material in a liquid phase with a flash point at or above 37.8 °C (100 °F) that is intentionally heated and offered for transportation or transported at or above its flash point in a bulk packaging
> **NFPA** 30. A **flammable** liquid is defined as a liquid. whose flash point does not exceed 100°F, when tested by closed-cup test methods, while a combustible liquid is one whose flash point is 100°F or higher, also when tested.

Flammable range - The % of vapor in air necessary for combustion to occur.

Flammable Solid - any material, other than an explosive, that is liable to cause fires through friction, retained heat from manufacturing or processing, or that can be ignited readily and when ignited burns so vigorously and persistently as to create a serious transportation hazard

Flame Impingement - the points where flames contact the surface of a container.

Flaring - Controlled burning of a high-pressure liquid or compressed gas in order to reduce or control the pressure and/or dispose of the product when transfer operations may be impractical.

Flashback - reignition of flammable liquid caused by exposure of its vapors to an ignition source.

Flash point - Lowest temperature at which a liquid or solid gives off vapor in such a concentration that, when the vapor combines with air near the surface of the liquid or solid, a flammable mixture is formed. Hence, the lower the flash point, the more flammable the product. Combustion does not necessarily continue. The flashpoint is lower than the ignition temperature.

Flash Powder- a pyrotechnic mixture containing an oxidizer and a metal such as aluminum. Used in theatrical and Fireworks displays and in law enforcement and military applications requiring sound and light without major explosive damage.

Flatcar - A freight car having a flat floor or deck laid on the underframe, with no sides or roof, designed for handling commodities not requiring protection from the weather.

Flowable - A pesticide formulation of finely ground particles of insoluble active ingredient suspended in a petroleum-based liquid combined with emulsifiers; flowables are mixed with water for final application.

FMC - Field Medical Card

FOG - Field Operations Guide

Fog - Liquid particles dispersed in air. A spray of very small pesticide-laden droplets that remain suspended in the air.

Fogging - The application of a pesticide in the form of a mist with particles in the 1-50 micron size range

Food Unit - Functional Unit within the Service Branch of the Logistics Section responsible for providing meals for incident personnel.

Formula - The molecular composition of a chemical compound written in scientific symbols. Water is H_2O; hydrochloric acid is HCl.

Formulation - The "form" a product is in in, i.e., dust granules

Freeze - To change from a liquid state to a solid state.

Freezing point – The temperature at which a material turns into its solid phase.

Frostbite - Injury caused to skin or other tissue by very cold materials. The medical consequences are similar to those caused by burns.

Froth-over - a steady, slow frothing over the rim of a tank without the sudden violent action that occurs in a boilover.

FTIR - Fourier Transform Infrared spectrometer

Fuel - a material that is oxidized to produce energy.

Fulminates—Compounds containing the Cyanate (CNO-) group. Fulminates like mercury fulminate are highly friction sensitive explosives used in primers.

Fume - a solid condensation particulate, usually of a vaporized metal.

Fumes - A general term for vapors, gases, or smoke.

Fumigant - A substance or mixture of substances which produce a gas vapor, fume or smoke intended to destroy insects, rodents, or bacteria. Lethal pesticide in the form of a gas or a liquid that rapidly becomes a gas when applied.

Fuming liquid - Emits gas (or vapor) that either mix or react with the moisture in the air to form a visible cloud.

Function - Function refers to the five major activities in ICS - Command, Operations, Planning, Logistics, and Finance/Administration. The term function is also used when describing the activity involved, e.g., the planning function. A sixth function, Intelligence, may be established, if required, to meet incident management needs.

Fungicide - A pesticide used for control of fungi.

Fungus - A general term used to denote a group of eukaryotic protist, including mushrooms, yeasts, rusts, molds, smuts, etc., which are characterized by the absence of a rigid cell wall composed of chitin, mannans, and sometimes cellulose.

Fusible Plugs - a safety relief device in the form of a plug of a low melting metal. The plugs close the safety relief device channel under normal conditions, and are intended to yield or melt at a set temperature to permit the escape of gas. Fusible Plugs normally melt between 158-165° but may be as high as 212°

G

g/Kg - Grams per Kilogram. A measurement used in experimental testing to indicate the dose of a test substance in grams, given for each Kilogram of the test subject's body weight.

g/L - Grams per liter.

G-Series Nerve Agents - Include tabun (GA), sarin (GB), soman (GD), and GF that are members of a class of compounds that are more lethal and quicker acting than mustard. They act rapidly and may be absorbed through the skin or the respiratory tract. Exposure to a lethal dose may cause death in as little as several minutes. These less persistent agents are used to cause immediate casualties and to create a short-term respiratory hazard on the battlefield.

GA – Tabun   Organophosphorus Nerve Agent.

GAO - General Accounting Office

Gamma Radiation - A highly penetrating type of nuclear radiation, similar to x-radiation, except that it comes from within the nucleus of an atom, and, in general, has a shorter wavelength.

Gamma Rays - Electromagnetic radiations of high energy photons, originating in atomic nuclei and accompanying many nuclear reactions. They can penetrate deeply into body tissue and many materials. Shielding against gamma radiation requires thick layers of dense materials, such as lead. Gamma rays are potentially lethal to humans.

Gas - A state of matter in which the material can expand and contract in response to pressure or temperature. Has no defined shape or form. Takes the shape of the container.

Gastrointestinal- pertaining to the stomach and intestine

GB – Sarin- Organophosphorus Nerve Agent.

GCC - Gulf Cooperation Council

GD – Soman- Organophosphorus Nerve Agent

GDP - Gross Domestic Product

Gauge Pressure - the pressure read on a gauge which does not take atmospheric pressure into account [psig] (pounds per square inch gauge).

Geiger-Mueller Counter - A radiation detection and measuring instrument. It consists of a gas-filled tube containing electrodes, between which there is an electrical voltage but no current flowing. When ionizing radiation passes through the tube, a short, intense pulse of current passes from the negative electrode to the positive electrode and is measured or counted. The number of pulses per second measures the intensity of radiation.

General Service (tank cars). Refers to non-pressure/low pressure (<100psi.) tank cars used for a wide variety of liquid products. Most often refers to DOT 111 specification tank cars.

General Staff - A group of incident management personnel organized according to function and reporting to the Incident Commander. The General Staff normally consists of the Operations Section Chief, Planning Section Chief, Logistics Section Chief, and Finance/Administration Section Chief.

General-Use Pesticide - Pesticides that have been designated for use by the general public as well as by licensed or certified applicators. General-use pesticides usually have minimal hazards.

Germinalaplasia - lack of development of egg and sperm cells

GF - Organophosphorus Nerve Agent cyclohexylmethylphosphonofluoridate,

GHS or Globally Harmonized Standards- Standards for information on hazardous materials. After June 1, 2015 all Safety Data Sheets and Labels must meet the GHS standards outlined in 29CFR1910.1200—The Hazcom Standard

GI - Gastrointestinal; gut.

GI or GIT - Gastrointestinal tract.

GIS - Geographic Information System

Glanders A contagious bacterial disease that causes pneumonia and inflammation in horses and other equines. Has been weaponized by several countries and was reportedly used by German Agents on horses shipped to Europe during World War I.

Glomerular - pertaining to a tuft or cluster, as of blood vessels or nerve fibers

gpm - Gallons per minute

Gondola Car - The common gondola car is a freight car with low sides and ends, a solid floor and no roof. It is used mainly for transportation of coal, iron, and steel products and other lading not requiring protection from the weather. Special types of gondola cars are built with high sides, removable covers, and other attachments for some specialized service.

Gouges - Indentations caused by contact with a sharp chisel-like object. Tank or weld metal is removed by the contact and the tank thickness is reduced.

Gram - A measure of weight in the metric system. One ounce equals 28.4 grams.

Gram Stain - A staining procedure used in classifying bacteria. A bacterial smear on a slide is stained with a purple basic triphenyl methane dye, usually crystal violet, in the presence of iodine/potassium iodide. The cells are then rinsed with alcohol or other solvent, and then counterstained, usually with safranin. The bacteria then appear purple or red according to their ability to keep the purple stain when rinsed with alcohol. This property is related to the composition of the bacterial cell wall.

Gram-Negative - Refers to the inability of many bacteria to retain crystal violet or similar stain through the standard Gram stain procedure. They show only the red counterstain.

Gram-Positive - Refers to the ability of many bacteria to retain crystal violet or similar stain through the standard Gram stain procedure. They retain a purple color.

Granules - A small sand like particle which carries/containers a chemical

Granulocytopenia - Decrease in white cells of the granulocyte series in the bloodstream.

Gray (Gy) - The International System of Units of absorbed dose. One Gy is equal to an absorbed dose of 1 J kg-1 (100 rad).

GREGG - Graves Registration

Gross Weight - the weight of a trailer together with the weight of its entire contents.

Ground Support Unit - Functional Unit within the Support Branch of the Logistics Section responsible for the fueling, maintaining, and repairing of vehicles, and the transportation of personnel and supplies.

Group - Groups are established to divide the incident into functional areas of operation. Groups are composed of resources assembled to perform a special function not necessarily within a single geographic division. (See Division.) Groups are located between Branches (when activated) and Resources in the Operations Section.

Gun Powder—Mixtures of Potassium Nitrate, Sulfur and Carbon. The first explosive, gun powder is still used today for fireworks and muzzle loading rifles.

H

Half-life - the time in which the concentration of a substance will be reduced by half Radioactive decay is measured in half-lives. One half-life is the amount of time it takes for a radioactive material to lose half of its initial radioactivity. The time required for an unstable element or nuclide to lose one half of its radioactive intensity in the form of alpha, beta, and gamma radiation. It is a constant for each radioactive element or nuclide. Half-lives vary from a small fraction of a second for some artificially produced radioactive elements to many millions of years. For example, the half-life of Uranium 235 is 10,000,000 years.

Halon - A class of simple hydrocarbon derivatives in which bromine, chlorine and fluorine are substituted for some or all of the hydrogen atoms. These compounds are used mainly as fire-extinguishing gases, the two best known being Halon 1211 (CF_2BrCl) and Halon 1301

Halogenated Hydrocarbon - The haloalkanes (also known as halogenoalkanes or alkyl halides) are a group of chemical compounds, derived from alkanes containing one or more halogens.

Hazard - Something that is potentially dangerous or harmful, often the root cause of an unwanted outcome. A potential risk or danger.

Hazard Warning - The words, pictures, and symbols, or combination thereof, that appear on a label and indicate the hazards of the substance in the container.

Hazardous chemicals - The Occupational Safety and Health Administration (OSHA) uses this term to denote any chemical that would be a risk to employees if an exposure occurred in the work place. This group (Hazardous Chemicals) covers a broader group of chemicals than the other lists. A chemical for which there is statistically significant evidence based on at least one study conducted in accordance with established scientific principles that acute or chronic health effects may occur in exposed employees. The term "health hazard" includes chemicals that are carcinogens, toxic or highly toxic agents, reproductive toxins, irritants, corrosives, sensitizers, hepatotoxins, nephrotoxins, neurotoxins, agents that act on the hematopoietic system, and agents that damage the lungs, skin, eyes, or mucous membranes. You can expand this definition to include chemicals that also pose physical hazards. A chemical is a physical hazard if it has flammable, combustible, explosive, oxidizing, pyrophoric or reactive properties, or if it is an organic peroxide or compressed gas.

Hazard Class - A group of materials, as designated by the Department of Transportation, that share a common major hazardous property such as radioactivity or flammability.

Hazardous materials - This term is utilized by the Department of Transportation (DOT) to denote materials in nine hazard classes of which divisions referred to as classifications exist. Any substance capable of causing harm to people, animals, property or the environment.

Hazardous Materials Response Team (HMRT) - A team of specially trained personnel who respond to a hazardous materials incident. The team performs various response actions including assessment, firefighting, rescue, and containment; they are not responsible for cleanup operations following the incident.

Hazardous substances - This term is used by the Environmental Protection Agency (EPA) for chemicals which if released into the environment above a certain amount. They must be reported and depending on the threat or danger to the environment may require or authorize Federal intervention. A list of EPA Hazardous Substances is found in 40 CFR, Part 302, Table 302.4.

Hazardous wastes - This term relates to materials that have been discarded and are regulated under the Resource Conservation and Recovery Act (RCRA) detailed in 40 CFR Part 261.33. Wastes are classified as "Hazardous" if they appear on EPA's "listed wastes" charts or meet the definition of "characteristic wastes" in terms of Ignitability, Corrosivity, Reactivity, or Toxicity. Hazardous Wastes are regulated in transit by the Department of Transportation (DOT).

HAZMAT - Hazardous Materials

Hazmat Incident - Actual or potential unplanned release of a hazardous material.

HAZWOPER - Name given to the 29CFR 1910.120 regulation entitled Hazardous Waste Operation and Emergency Response.

HDBTDC - Hard and Deeply Buried Target Defeat Capability

Head Shield - A form of protection given to the ends, heads, of tank cars. Head shield may be retrofitted to older cars in the form of a large plate on the outside of the tank car, or integrated into the car during new construction through a thicker head tank section.

Heat Affected Zone - The area in the undisturbed tank metal next to where weld material is deposited. This zone is less ductile than either the weld or the base metal due to the effect of the heat from the welding operation.

Health Hazard
> Acute - immediate toxic effects
> Chronic - persistent or prolonged injury
> Delayed - toxic effect occurring after a lapse of time

Heat Cramps - An illness due, in part, to excessive loss of salt during sweating resulting in painful muscle spasms in the extremities, back and abdomen.

Heat Exhaustion - An illness due to circulatory failure in which venous blood returned to the heart is significantly reduced; fainting may result. This failure is caused because the individual's blood supply is not adequate to serve both heat regulation and other bodily needs.

Heat of Dilution—The amount of heat given off when two materials are mixed to form a solution. For example, mixing water and sulfuric acid will result in the release of large amounts of heat which may boil the solution.

Heat of Neutralization- The amount of heat given off when acids and bases are mixed

Heat of Reaction- The amount of heat given off when two or more chemicals react to form products—also used to describe the heat given off during polymerization reactions.

Heat of Solution—The amount of heat given off or taken up when one chemical is dissolved in another. For example, mixing solid ammonium chloride in water will cause the resulting mixture to get cold where-as dissolving solid sodium hydroxide in water will cause a large temperature rise.

Heat of Vaporization-The amount of heat required to cause a material to go from the liquid state to the vapor state.

Heat Strain - The natural, physiological response reaction of the body to the application of heat stress.

Heat Stress - The relative amount of thermal strain from the environment.

Heat Stroke - An illness due to the body temperature reaching a level where sweating stops. The body temperature can then rise to critical levels causing tissue damage and death.

Helibase - The main location for parking, fueling, maintenance, and loading of helicopters operating in support of an incident. It is usually located at or near the incident Base.

Helispot - Any designated location where a helicopter can safely take off and land. Some helispots may be used for loading of supplies, equipment, or personnel.

Hematopoietic System - The blood-forming organs of the body, including bone marrow and the spleen.

HEPA - High-Efficiency Particulate Air.

Hepatotoxin - A chemical that can cause liver damage (e.g., carbon tetrachloride).

Highly Toxic. A chemical that falls within any of the following categories:
   a) A chemical that has a median lethal dose (LD50) of 50mg or less per kg of body weight when administered orally to albino rats weighing between 200 g and 300 g each
   b) A chemical that has a median lethal dose (LD50) of 200 mg or less per kg of body weight when administered by continuous contact for 24 hours (or less if death occurs within 24 hours) with the bare skin of albino rabbits weighing between 2 kg and 3 kg each
   c) A chemical that has a median lethal concentration (LD50) in air of 200 parts per million by volume or less of gas or vapor, or 2 mg per L or less of mist, fume, or dust, when administered by continuous inhalation for 1 hour (or less if death occurs within 1 hour) to albino rats weighing between 200 g and 300 g each

Hematoma - localized collection of blood, usually clotted, in an organ, space, or tissue, due to a break in the wall of the blood vessel

Hematopoietic - Pertaining to production and development of blood cells.

Hematopoietic system - Includes the blood and blood producing tissues.

Hematotoxins - Toxins that affect the circulatory system.

Hematuria - blood in the urine

Hemoconcentration - A relative increase in the number of red blood cells, usually resulting from a decrease in the volume of plasma.

Hemoglobinuria - presence of free red blood cells and its appearance in the plasma

Hemolysis - separation of hemoglobin from red blood cells and its appearance in the plasma

Hemolytic - pertaining to or characterized by hemolysis

HEPA - High--efficiency particulate air filter. Also called "absolute" filter. Has a minimum 99.97% removal of 0.03 micron or larger particles.

Hepatic - pertaining to the liver

Hepatotoxins - Toxins that effect the liver.

Herbicide - A pesticide used for the control of weeds

HHA - Hand Held Immunochromatographic Assays

Hierarchy of Command - See Chain of Command.

Highly Flammable - Defined as the equivalent of NFPA Flammability Hazard Class 3 or GHS Class 1.

HMRT - Hazardous Materials Response Team

HMTD Hexamethylene Triperoxide Diamine. A high explosive used as a Primer especially in mining operations

HMX—a Nitroamine High Explosive related to RDX—a military explosive

Hopper Car - A freight car, either open or closed, designed for handling bulk commodities such as coal or grain. Hopper cars have floor sheets that slope from the car sides and ends to form a series of pockets or hoppers, which when opened can discharge the bulk lading by gravity through hopper doors operated from outside the car.

Hormone - A chemical produced in the cells of a plant or animal that produces changes in cells in another part of the organism's structure.

Hot Tapping - An offensive response technique used by highly qualified specialists for welding on and cutting holes through liquid and/or compressed gas tanks, vessels or piping for the purposes of relieving the internal pressure and/or removing the product.

Hot zone - Area immediately surrounding a dangerous goods incident which extends far enough to prevent adverse effects from released dangerous goods to personnel outside the zone. This zone is also referred to as exclusion zone or restricted zone.

HSPD-5 - Homeland Security Presidential Directive-5

HTH - High Test Hypochlorite

Human Immunodeficiency Virus (HIV) - The condition of having antibodies indicating the presence of HIV; the pathogen that causes Acquired Immune Deficiency Syndrome (AIDS).

Humectant - moistening or diluent substance

Hump Yard - A railroad classification yard in which the classification (or sorting) of cars is accomplished by pushing them over a summit (the "hump") beyond which they run by gravity into the correct track.

HVAC - An acronym for Heating, Ventilating, and Air Conditioning systems.

Hydrocarbon - An organic compound containing only carbon hydrogen and often occurring in petroleum, natural gas, coal, and bitumens.

Hydrolysis - A term used when chemicals are decomposed with water. Vapors may be given off.

Hydrolyzed - Refers to a compound which has undergone chemical reaction with water; hydrolysis is the reaction of a particular compound with water to form new chemical compounds ("reaction products").

Hydrophilic - Water loving or attracted by water.

Hydrophobic - Water fearing or repelled by water.

Hygroscopic - the ability of a substance to absorb moisture from the air.

Hyperactivity - abnormally increased activity

Hyperalimentation - ingestion or administration of a greater than optimal amount of nutrients

Hyperbilirubinemia - an excess of bilirubin in the blood

Hypercalcemia - excess of calcium in the blood

Hyperemia - Redness of the skin.

Hypergolic - Any substance that spontaneously ignites upon contact with another.

Hypergolic Mixture - the property by which a fuel and an oxidizer will ignite on contact with each other without the need of an outside source of ignition.

Hyperparathyroidism - abnormally increased activity of the parathyroid glands which affects and is affected by serum calcium levels

Hyperpyrexia - a highly elevated body temperature

Hyperreflexia - exaggeration of reflexes

Hypersalivation - excessive secretion of saliva

Hypertension - persistently high arterial blood pressure

Hyperthermia – Condition of increased body temperature, above 98.6 degree F.

Hypothermia – Condition of decreased body temperature, below 98.6 degree F.

Hypobilirubinemia - abnormally low levels of bilirubin in the blood

Hypocalcaemia - abnormal reduction of blood calcium levels

Hypotension - Low blood pressure; if blood pressure is too low, shock and death may occur.

Hypovolemic- pertaining to an abnormally decreased volume of circulating fluid (plasma) in the body

Hypovolemic shock - Insufficient blood volume to maintain adequate tissue oxygenation and aerobic metabolism.

Hypoxemia (hypoxia) - Insufficient oxygen in the circulatory system to adequately supply tissue cells. May be caused by lack of oxygen, inadequate hemoglobin to carry oxygen, or interference with transfer of oxygen to the cells.

Hypoxia - low oxygen content or tension; deficiency of oxygen in the inspired air

I

IAEA - International Atomic Energy Agency

IAP - Incident Action Plan

IARC - International Agency on Research on Cancer. Publishes "Monographs on the Evaluation of the Carcinogenic Risk of Chemicals to Man," one of the publications used to determine the cancer risk of a chemical.

IATA - International Air Transport Association

IC - Incident Commander

IC or UC - Incident Command or Unified Command

ICAM - Improved Chemical Agent Monitor

ICAO - International Civil Aviation Organization

ICBM - Intercontinental Ballistic Missile (Range - greater than 5,500 kilometers)

ICP - Incident Command Post

ICS - An acronym for Incident Command System.

ICt50 - Inhalation dose of a chemical agent (vapor or aerosol) that produces a given, defined level of "incapacitation" in 50 percent of the exposed subjects (see **ED50**, and consider "incapacitation" as the effect). NOTE: There is no general consensus on a military definition of incapacitation. It can refer to behavioral manifestations, physiologic endpoints, or individual combat effectiveness, all of which may vary depending upon the task the individual soldier is expected to accomplish.

ID50 - Dose of a liquid chemical agent needed to produce "incapacitation" in 50 percent of the exposed subjects (see note under ICt50).

IDLH - Immediately Dangerous to Life and Health. An atmospheric concentration of any toxic, corrosive or asphyxiant substance that poses an immediate threat to life or would cause irreversible or delayed adverse health effects or would interfere with an individual's ability to escape from a dangerous atmosphere.

IED-Improvised Explosive Device. Explosive devices other than military ordnance typically used in terrorist attacks or in guerilla warfare conflicts.

Ignition source - Includes heat, sparks, flames, static electricity and friction. Ignition sources should always be eliminated.

Ignition Temperature - The minimum temperature to which a material must be raised before it will burn. The ignition temperature is higher than the flashpoint.

IGR - Insect Growth Regulator

ILEA - International Law Enforcement Academy

ILT - Insect Lighting Trap

Immiscible - Material that does not mix readily with water. Materials that are insoluble in each other.

IMO - International Maritime Organization

IMT - Incident Management Team

Incapacitating Agent - A chemical agent that produces a temporary, disabling condition that persists for hours to days after exposure has ceased. Complete recovery of incapacitating agent casualties is expected without medical treatment.

Incendiary Device - Any mechanical, electrical, or chemical device used intentionally to initiate combustion and start a fire.

Incident - An occurrence or event, natural or human-caused, that requires an emergency response to protect life or property. Incidents can, for example, include major disasters, emergencies, terrorist attacks, terrorist threats, wild land and urban fires, floods, hazardous materials spills, nuclear accidents, aircraft accidents, earthquakes, hurricanes, tornadoes, tropical storms, war-related disasters, public health and medical emergencies, and other occurrences requiring an emergency response.

Incident Action Plan (IAP) - An oral or written plan containing general objectives reflecting the overall strategy for managing an incident. It may include the identification of operational resources and assignments. It may also include attachments that provide direction and important information for management of the incident during one or more operational periods.

Incident Base - Location at the incident where the primary Logistics functions are coordinated and administered. (Incident name or other designator will be added to the term Base.) The Incident Command Post may be collocated with the Base. There is only one Base per incident.

Incident Command Post (ICP) - The field location at which the primary tactical-level, on-scene incident command functions are performed. The ICP may be collocated with the incident base or other incident facilities and is normally identified by a green rotating or flashing light.

Incident Command System (ICS) - A standardized on-scene emergency management construct specifically designed to provide for the adoption of an integrated organizational structure that reflects the complexity and demands of single or multiple incidents, without being hindered by jurisdictional boundaries. ICS is the combination of facilities, equipment, personnel, procedures, and communications operating within a common organizational structure, designed to aid in the management of resources during incidents. It is used for all kinds of emergencies and is applicable to small as well as large and complex incidents. ICS is used by various jurisdictions and functional agencies, both public and private, to organize field-level incident management operations. The OSHA Hazardous Waste Operations and Emergency Response regulations (29 CFR 1910.120(q)(3)(ii)) require that an ICS be implemented by the senior emergency response official on the scene. See Appendix C, Section 6, of the OSHA rule for more information on ICS.

Incident Commander (IC) - The individual responsible for all incident activities, including the development of strategies and tactics and the ordering and the release of resources. The IC has overall authority and responsibility for conducting incident operations and is responsible for the management of all incident operations at the incident site.

Incident Communications Center - The location of the Communications Unit and the Message Center.

Incident Complex - See Complex.

Incident Management Team (IMT) - The IC and appropriate Command and General Staff personnel assigned to an incident.

Incident Objectives - Statements of guidance and direction necessary for the selection of appropriate strategy(ies), and the tactical direction of resources. Incident objectives are based on realistic expectations of what can be accomplished when all allocated resources have been effectively deployed. Incident objectives must be achievable and measurable, yet flexible enough to allow for strategic and tactical alternatives.

Incident of National Significance - Based on criteria established in HSPD-5 (paragraph 4), an actual or potential high-impact event that requires a coordinated and effective response by and appropriate combination of Federal, State, local, tribal, nongovernmental, and/or private-sector entities in order to save lives and minimize damage, and provide the basis for long-term community recovery and mitigation activities. (Source - National Response Plan)

Incident Support Organization - Includes any off-incident support provided to an incident. Examples would be Agency Dispatch centers, Airports, Mobilization Centers, etc.

Incident Types - Incidents are categorized by five types based on complexity. Type 5 incidents are the least complex and Type 1 the most complex.

Incompatible - The term applied to two substances to indicate that one material cannot be mixed with the other without the possibility of a dangerous reaction.

Inert Ingredients - Materials in the pesticide formulation that are not the active ingredient. Some inert ingredients may be toxic or hazardous to people.

Infectious Substances - a viable microorganism, or its toxin, that causes or may cause disease in humans or animals. Infectious substance and etiologic agent are synonymous. Class 6 (Poison)

Infestation - A troublesome invasion of pests within an area such as a building, greenhouse, agricultural crop or landscaped location.

Inhalation - Breathing a chemical into the lung. The most common route of exposure to hazardous materials.

Inhibit - To prevent something from happening, such as a biochemical reaction within the tissues of a plant or animal.

Inhibited - Containing a small amount of another substance that is included to prevent the first (bulk) material from reacting with itself or other things in its environment.

Inhibitor - A substance that is used to retard the rate of a chemical reaction. Most commonly, inhibitors are associated with monomers to prevent polymerization.

Infectious - Caused by infection or capable of causing infection. Transmitted from one person to another, usually through the air breathed; Able to infect others; Spreading quickly from one person to another.

Initial Action - The actions taken by resources that are the first to arrive at an incident site.

Initial Response - Resources initially committed to an incident.

Inorganic - Compounds which lack carbon. Exceptions are carbon monoxide and carbon dioxide which are classed as inorganic.

Insect Growth Regulator (IGR) - A type of pesticide used for control of certain insects. Insect growth regulators disrupt the normal process of development from immature to mature life stages.

Insecticide - A pesticide used for the control insects. Some insecticides are also labeled for control of ticks, mites, spiders and other arthropods.

Insidious - Having a gradual cumulative effect.

Insoluble - Material does not dissolve in water or other stated solvent.

Instability - The quality of being unstable; A state that is not in equilibrium, or in which a small change has a large irreversible effect. Materials that decompose spontaneously, polymerize, or otherwise self-react are generally considered unstable. They do not need to mix with other chemicals to react. The term instability is often used interchangeably with the term chemical reactivity.

Intelligence Officer – In the IC System, the intelligence officer is responsible for managing internal information, intelligence, and operational security requirements supporting incident management activities. These may include information security and operational security activities, as well as the complex task of ensuring that sensitive information of all types (e.g., classified information, law enforcement sensitive information, proprietary information, or export-controlled information) is handled in a way that not only safeguards the information, but also ensures that it gets to those who need access to it to perform their missions effectively and safely.

Interstitial Pneumonia - a chronic form of pneumonia with increase of the interstitial tissue and decrease of the proper lung tissue

Inversion - An atmospheric condition caused by a layer of warm air preventing cool air trapped beneath it from rising, thus holding down pollutants that could otherwise be dispersed.

Invertebrate - Any animal having an external skeleton or shell, such as insects, spiders, mites, worms, nematodes, snails and slugs.

Ion - An atom or molecule that carries a positive or negative electrical charge due to losing or gaining electrons through a chemical reaction.

Ionic Compound – A molecule that exists as a pair (or more) of ionized subparts which may dissociate in solution. In most ionic compounds, the positively charged portion consists of metal cations or positively charged species such as Ammonium (NH_4+) ions and the negatively charged portion is an anion or polyatomic ion.

Ionizing Radiation - Electromagnetic radiation (gamma or X-ray) or particulate radiation (alpha particles, beta particles, neutrons, etc.) capable of producing ions, i.e., electrically charged particles, directly or indirectly, in its passage through matter.

IPDS - Improved Point Detection System

IPM - Integrated Pest Management

IRBM - Intermediate Range Ballistic Missile (Range - 3,000 to 5,000 kilometers)

Iritis - Inflammation of the iris with accompanying pain, photophobia, lacrimation, and diminution with transfer of oxygen to the cells.

Irritant - A substance that can cause irritation of the skin, eyes, or respiratory system. Typically will inflame living tissue by chemical action at the site of contact, causing pain or swelling. Effects may be acute from a single high level exposure, or chronic from repeated low-level exposures to such compounds as chlorine, nitrogen dioxide, and nitric acid.

Isomer - A material with the same chemical composition (i.e. kind and number of elements) as another material but with a different arrangement of those elements. For example, n-butyl alcohol and t-butyl alcohol are isomers of one another.

Isotonia - a solution having the same effective osmotic pressure as the body fluid to which it is compared

Isotope - The term isotope defines atoms that have the same number of protons but a different number of neutrons; that is, they are atoms of the same element that have different masses. Their atomic number (proton number) is the same, but their mass numbers (the total number of protons and neutrons in the nucleus) vary. Forms of the same element having identical chemical properties but differing in their atomic masses and in their nuclear properties.

J

Jaundice - syndrome characterized by hyperbilirubinemia and deposition of bile pigment in the skin, resulting in yellow appearance of the patient

JBPDS - Joint Biological Point Detection System

JIC - Joint Information Center A facility established to coordinate all incident-related public information activities. It is the central point of contact for all news media at the scene of the incident. Public information officials from all participating agencies should collocate at the JIC.

JIS - Joint Information System - Integrates incident information and public affairs into a cohesive organization designed to provide consistent, coordinated, timely information during crisis or incident operations. The mission of the JIS is to provide a structure and system for developing and delivering coordinated interagency messages; developing, recommending, and executing public information plans and strategies on behalf of the Incident Commander; advising the Incident Commander concerning public affairs issues that could affect a response effort; and controlling rumors and inaccurate information that could undermine public confidence in the emergency response effort.

JSLIST - Joint Service Lightweight Integrated Suit Technology

Jurisdiction - A range or sphere of authority. Public agencies have jurisdiction at an incident related to their legal responsibilities and authority. Jurisdictional authority at an incident can be political or geographical (e.g., city, county, tribal, State, or Federal boundary lines) or functional (e.g., law enforcement, public health).

Jurisdictional Agency - The agency having jurisdiction and responsibility for a specific geographical area, or a mandated function.

Juvenile Hormone - A chemical which regulates the development of insects.

JVAP - Joint Vaccine Acquisition Program

JWCO - Joint Warfighting Capability Objective

K

Kg or kg - Abbreviation for kilogram, a measure of weight in the metric system.

Kinds of Resources - Describe what the resource is (e.g., medic, firefighter, planning section chief, helicopters, ambulances, combustible gas indicators, bulldozers).

km - Abbreviation for Kilometer

Knapsack Sprayer - A small portable sprayer carried on the back of the person making a pesticide application. Some knapsack sprayers are hand-operated and others are powered by small gasoline engines.

KPH - Kilometers Per Hour

L

Label - Written or printed material which pertains to the composition of uses of, precautions for use and limits of any chemical. It is the definitive guide for pesticide use and its compliance is mandated by law.

Lachrymator (or lacrimator) - a substance which increases the flow of tears. A lachrymatory agent or lachrymator (from lacrima meaning "a tear" in Latin;) is a chemical compound that stimulates the corneal nerves in the eyes to cause tearing, pain, and even blindness.

Lacrimation- secretion and discharge of tears

Lachrymator - A chemical or material that causes the production of tears.

Landing Zone - See Helispot.

Larva - The immature form of insects that undergo metamorphosis (plural - larvae).

Laryngospasm - spasmodic closure of the larynx

Larynx- the muscular and cartilage structure situated at the top of the trachea

Lassa Fever - An acute illness caused by the RNA containing Arenavirus. This is also classified as one of the viral hemorrhagic fevers. Transmission may be from infected rodents, contact with infected body fluids, or person-to-person contact. The incubation period is 6 to 21 days. Headache, sore throat, cough, chest pain, abdominal pain, vomiting, diarrhea and fever are frequent symptoms.

Lassitude - weakness; exhaustion

Latency - a state of seeming inactivity. A period after exposure to a chemical or biological agent before symptoms of exposure appear.

LBE - Load Bearing Equipment

LC50 - Concentration of a toxic material which kills half of the test population in a specified time. The lethal concentration of a pesticide in the air or in a body of water that will kill half of a test animal population. LC50 values are given in micrograms per milliliter of air or water (ug/ml).

LCL - Liquid Control Line

Lct50 (Median Lethal Concentration) - A dosage of a substance by inhalation that results in death in 50 percent of the exposed population; the vapor or aerosol exposure (Ct, concentration X time) that is lethal (L) to 50% of the exposed population.

LD50 - Dose of a toxic material which kills half of the test population in a specified time. The lethal dose of a material that will kill half of a test animal population. LD50 values are given in milligrams per kilogram of test animal body weight (mg/kg). Published LD50 values also specify the route of exposure and the test animal used. This is important information because some animals are more sensitive to specific toxins than others.

Leachate - Material that pollutes water as it seeps through solid waste.

Leaching - The process by which water dissolves nutrient chemicals or contaminants and carries them away, or moves them to a lower layer. The process by which some pesticides move down through the soil, usually by being dissolved in water, with the possibility of reaching groundwater.

Leader - The ICS title for an individual responsible for a Task Force, Strike Team, or functional Unit.

LEL, LFL - The lower flammable limit (LFL) or lower explosive limit (LEL) is the minimum concentration of vapor to air below which the propagation of a flame will not occur in the presence of an ignition source.

LEPC - An acronym for Local Emergency Planning Committee.

Lesion - a pathological or traumatic discontinuity of tissue or loss of function of a part

Lethal - Capable of causing death. Deadly, Fatal

Lethal Dose (50/30) - The dose of radiation expected to cause death within 30 days to 50% of those exposed without medical treatment. The generally accepted range from 400-500 rem received over a short period of time.

Leukocytosis - Above normal increase of white blood cells.

Leukopenia - Less than normal number of white blood cells. Reduction in the number of leukocytes in the blood.

Level A – Level of Chemical Protective Clothing required at an incident. This is normally SCBA plus fully encapsulating chemical resistant clothing. Note that a Level A suit is vapor proof but is subject to permeation of material on the surface.

Level B - Level of Chemical Protective Clothing required at an incident. This is normally SCBA plus chemical resistant clothing (splash proof).

Level C – Level of Chemical Protective Clothing required at an incident. This is normally Full- or half-face respirator plus chemical resistant clothing (splash proof).

Level D - Level of Chemical Protective Clothing required at an incident. This is normally Coveralls with no respiratory protection.

Lewisite - a lethal war agent which is a vesicant, lacrimator and lung irritant

Liaison - A form of communication for establishing and maintaining mutual understanding and cooperation.

Liaison Officer (LNO) - A member of the Command Staff responsible for coordinating with representatives from cooperating and assisting agencies. The Liaison Officer may have Assistants.

Light Weight - The empty weight of a rail car including its trucks and any other appurtenances considered standard to the car. The light weight is stenciled in every freight car in conjunction with the capacity and load limit and is abbreviated LT. WT.

Liter - A measure of volume (usually liquid) in the metric system; a little more than a quart.

LNBCRS - Lightweight Nuclear Biological and Chemical Reconnaissance System

Load Limit - The maximum weight of lading that can be loaded into a railcar. For cars meeting the AAR standard design criteria the load limit is equal to the maximum allowable gross weight on rails less the light weight of the car. Load limit is stenciled on every freight car and is abbreviated LD. LT.

LOAEL - The Lowest Observed Adverse Effect Level, i.e., the lowest dose which produces an observable adverse effect.

Local Government - A county, municipality, city, town, township, local public authority, school district, special district, intrastate district, council of governments (regardless of whether the council of governments is incorporated as a nonprofit corporation under State law), regional or interstate government entity, or agency or instrumentality of a local government; an Indian tribe or authorized tribal organization, or in Alaska a Native village or Alaska Regional Native Corporation; a rural community, unincorporated town or village, or other public entity. See Section 2 (10), Homeland Security Act of 2002, Pub. L. 107-296, 116 Stat. 2135 (2002).

Logistics - Providing resources and other services to support incident management. Logistics Section - The Section responsible for providing facilities, services, and materials for the incident.

Lowest-Observed Adverse Effect Level (LOAEL) - The lowest exposure level at which there are statistically or biologically significant increases in frequency or severity of adverse effects between the exposed population and its appropriate control group.

LRBSDS - Long Range Biological Standoff Detection System

LSD Lysergic acid diethylamide is a synthetic hallucinogenic (psychedelic) compound. It has been tested as an incapacitating agent.

Lymphadenitis - Inflammation of lymph nodes, usually caused by a focus of infection distal to the node.

M

m - An abbreviation for "meta". Referring to a particular arrangement of groups attached to a benzene molecule.

m3 - Cubic meter. A volume measurement in the metric system. One m3 is about 35.3 cubic feet, or 1.3 cubic yards.

M256-Series Chemical Agent Detector Kit - This kit is used at squad, crew or section level to detect and identify field concentrations of nerve, blister or blood agent vapors. The kit consists of 12 individually packaged samplers/detectors and a packet of M8 detector paper.

M8 Chemical Agent Detection Paper - A chemically treated, dye-impregnated paper, issued in a book of 25 sheets. It is designed to detect liquid V, G, and H agents. M8 paper will change colorsto identify non-persistent G-type nerve (yellow), V-type nerve (black or dark green), or blister (red) agents. It is included in the M256A I Kit and in the M18A2 Chemical Agent Detection Kit.

M9 Chemical Agent Detector Paper - The M9 self-adhesive paper attaches to most surfaces. The paper indicates the presence of a nerve agent (G or V) or a blister agent (H or L) by turning a red or reddish color.

Major Disaster - As defined under the Robert T. Stafford Disaster Relief and Emergency Assistance Act (42 U.S.C. 5122), a major disaster is any natural catastrophe (including any hurricane, tornado, storm, high water, wind-driven water, tidal wave, tsunami, earthquake, volcanic eruption, landslide, mudslide, snowstorm, or drought), or, regardless of cause, any fire, flood, or explosion, in any part of the United States, which in the determination of the President causes damage of sufficient severity and magnitude to warrant major disaster assistance under this Act to supplement the efforts and available resources of States, tribes, local governments, and disaster relief organizations in alleviating the damage, loss, hardship, or suffering caused thereby.

Malaise - a vague feeling of bodily discomfort

Management by Objective - A management approach that involves a four-step process for achieving the incident goal. The Management by Objectives approach includes the following - establishing overarching objectives; developing and issuing assignments, plans, procedures, and protocols; establishing specific, measurable objectives for various incident management functional activities and directing efforts to fulfill them, in support of defined strategic objectives; and documenting results to measure performance and facilitate corrective action.

Managers - Individuals within ICS organizational Units that are assigned specific managerial responsibilities, e.g., Staging Area Manager or Camp Manager.

Mania- a phase of mental disorder characterized by an expansive emotional state, elation, overtalkativeness, and increased motor activity

Marburg Virus - One of the RNA containing Filovirus family also classified in the viral hemorrhagic fever group. The incubation period is 3 to 9 days. The disease is contracted by skin or mucous membrane contact with blood or other tissues of infected monkeys or humans. The disease is manifested by headache, sore throat, muscle aches, chest pain, vomiting, diarrhea, skin rash, jaundice, easy bruising and bleeding.

Marine pollutant - Substances, articles or materials which, if released into the aquatic environment, may cause serious environmental damage.

MARK I Kit. -also called the **NAAK** Kit This kit consists of two syringes containing atropine and pralodoxime chloride to counteract exposure to organophosphate nerve agents.

Mass explosion - Explosion which affects almost the entire load virtually instantaneously.

Maximum Safe Storage Temperature - The maximum safe temperature at which a product can be stored. This temperature is well below the SADT.

MCTL - Militarily Critical Technologies List

MEADS - Medium Extended Air Defense System

Medical Unit - Functional Unit within the Service Branch of the Logistics Section responsible for the development of the Medical Emergency Plan, and for providing emergency medical treatment of incident personnel.

Melting point - Temperature at which a solid turns into its liquid phase. Solid materials with low melting points should not be stored in hot areas.

MES - Medical Equipment Set

Mesh - The term used to describe the number of wires per inch in a screen, such as one used to filter foreign particles out of spray solutions to keep nozzles from becoming clogged. Mesh is also the term used to describe the size of pesticide granules, pellets and dusts.

Message Center - The Message Center is part of the Incident Communications Center and is collocated or placed adjacent to it. It receives, records, and routes information about resources reporting to the incident, resource status, and administrative and tactical traffic.

Metastatic - pertaining to the transfer of disease from one organ or part to another not directly connected with it

Methemoglobin - An abnormal form of hemoglobin which will not carry oxygen in the blood.

Methemoglobinemia - presence of methemoglobin (oxidized hemoglobin) in the blood

mg - Milligram; a measure of weight in the metric system, one thousandth of a gram: 1 mg = 0.001 g = 1000 µg. The amount of material in about 2-3 grains of salt.

mg/kg - Milligrams per kilogram

mg/m3 - Milligrams per cubic meter. The mass in micrograms of a substance contained within a cubic meter of another substance or vacuum. This is the standard unit of measure for the mass density (concentration) of particles suspended in air; also sometimes used for the concentration of gases in air.

Microencapsulated - A pesticide formulation in which particles of the active ingredient are encased in plastic capsules; pesticide is released after application when the capsules break down.

Micron - A very small unit of measure - 1/1,000,000th of a meter

Miosis (or myosis) - The excessive smallness or contraction of the pupil of the eye. The pupil is unable to dilate and remains contracted; thus, performance of tasks, navigating on foot, identifying or engaging targets, or driving vehicles is practically impossible. Miosis is oftenaccompanied by pain, headaches, and pinpointing of the pupils.

Miscible - Material mixes with water or other stated material in any or all proportions. Capable of mixing in any ratio without separation of two phases.

Mist - Suspended liquid droplets in air caused by condensation or atomization. The particles are up to 100 microns in diameter.

Mitigation - The activities designed to reduce or eliminate risks to persons or property or to lessen the actual or potential effects or consequences of an incident. Mitigation measures may be implemented prior to, during, or after an incident. Mitigation measures are often informed by lessons learned from prior incidents. Mitigation involves ongoing actions to reduce exposure to, probability of, or potential loss from hazards. Measures may include zoning and building codes, floodplain buyouts, and analysis of hazard- related data to determine where it is safe to build or locate temporary facilities. Mitigation can include efforts to educate governments, businesses, and the public on measures they can take to reduce loss and injury.

Mixture - Material composed of more than one chemical compound or element mixed together, not necessarily in any fixed proportions and not with chemical bonding

ml - Millilter A metric unit used to measure capacity. One milliliter equals one cubic centimeter. One thousand milliliters equal one liter.

MLD - The estimated minimum lethal dose.

Mobilization - The process and procedures used by all organizations (Federal, State, local, and tribal) for activating, assembling, and transporting all resources that have been requested to respond to or support an incident.

Mobilization Center - An off-incident location at which emergency service personnel and equipment are temporarily located pending assignment, release, or reassignment.

Mode of Action - The way a pesticide reacts with a pest organism to destroy it.

Molecular weight - Total mass of any group of atoms bound together to act as a single unit.

Monitor - A self-supporting firefighting nozzle which can function unattended and delivers a large volume of fire suppressant material.

Monkey Pox Virus - A virus that causes a blister type rash in monkeys similar to small pox in man. The disease is endemic in Western and Central Africa and has infected humans in this geographic area. It may have the ability for person-to-person transmission. It causes swollen lymph nodes in the neck and groin areas.

Monomer - Material that makes polymers.

MOPP - Mission Oriented Protective Posture

MOPP Gear – A type of PPE worn by the military. There are different levels of protection.

- MOPP Level 0 — Protective mask worn in carrier, at side. Overgarments, gloves, and overboots accessible.
- MOPP Level 1 — Overgarments worn, chemical agent detectors worn, mask worn in carrier at side. Gloves and overboots readily accessible.
- MOPP Level 2 — Overgarments and overboots worn. Gloves and mask readily accessible.
- MOPP Level 3 — Mask, overgarments, and overboots worn. Gloves kept ready.
- MOPP Level 4 — All protection worn.

Mordant - a chemical that fixes a dye in or on a substance by combining with the dye to form an insoluble compound

Mortality - Proportion of deaths to the population of a region.

MPPCF - Million particles per cubic foot of air

MRBM - Medium Range Ballistic Missile (Range - 1,000 to 3,000 kilometers)

MSDS - Material safety data sheet. A worksheet required by the U.S. Occupational Safety and Health Administration (OSHA) containing information about hazardous chemicals in the workplace. MSDSs are used to fulfill part of the hazardous chemical inventory reporting requirements under the Emergency Planning and Community Right-to-Know Act. Contains information about the material such and health and safety information, first aid, physical and chemical properties, firefighting and other information.

MT - Metric Ton

MTCR - Missile Technology Control Regime

MTF - Medical Treatment Facility

MTO&E - Modified Table of Organization and Equipment

MTOPS - Million Theoretical Operations Per Second

Mucous membranes - A protective lining of cells found, for example, in the mouth, throat, nose, and other parts of the respiratory system.

Multiagency Coordination (MAC) - The coordination of assisting agency resources and support to emergency operations.

Multiagency Coordination Entity - A multiagency coordination entity functions within a broader multiagency coordination system. It may establish the priorities among incidents and associated resource allocations, deconflict agency policies, and provide strategic guidance and direction to support incident management activities.

Multiagency Coordination Systems (MACs) - Multiagency coordination systems provide the architecture to support coordination for incident prioritization, critical resource allocation, communications systems integration, and information coordination. The components of multiagency coordination systems include facilities, equipment, emergency operation centers (EOCs), specific multiagency coordination entities, personnel, procedures, and communications. These systems assist agencies and organizations to fully integrate the subsystems of the NIMS. Multijurisdictional Incident - An incident requiring action from multiple agencies that each have jurisdiction to manage certain aspects of an incident. In ICS, these incidents will be managed under Unified Command.

Mustard - The chemical Bis(2-chloroethyl) sulfide, CAS registry number 505-60-2, in pure form and in the various impure forms that may be found in munitions as well as field, industrial, or laboratory operations. These include Levinstein mustard (H), distilled mustard (HD), and closely related preparations. This standard is not meant to be applied to nitrogen mustards.

Mutagen - Substance causing genes in an organism to mutate or change.

Mutagenic - inducing genetic mutation

Mutagenicity - The cause of changes in cellular genetic material which may be passed on to subsequent generations of cells. When these changes occur in germ cells (i.e., sperm or ova), the mutations may be passed on to subsequent generations.

Mutual-Aid Agreement - Written agreement between agencies and/or jurisdictions that they will assist one another on request, by furnishing personnel, equipment, and/or expertise in a specified manner.

Mycotoxin - A fungal toxin. They can cause illness or death upon ingestion, skin contact or inhalation. They exhibit great stability and heat resistance. Mycotoxins are difficult to detect, to identify, and to decontaminate.

Mydriasis - Large or dilated pupils. Extreme dilation of the pupil.

Myelosuppression - suppression of the formation of bone marrow

N

N- - A symbol used in some chemical names indicating that the next section of the name refers to a chemical group attached to a nitrogen atom.

n- - An abbreviation for "normal". It refers to the arrangement of carbon atoms in a chemical molecule.

NOAEL - No Observable Adverse Effect Level.

N.O.I.B.N. - Means Not Otherwise Indexed By Name. Used in shipping descriptions of non regulated hazardous materials.

N.O.S. - Means Not Otherwise Specified. Used in shipping descriptions of regulated hazardous materials.

NA Identification Number - An acronym for North America. A four-digit number assigned to some chemicals found in transport in North America.

NAAK - Nerve Agent Antidote Kit also called the **MARK I Kit.** This kit consists of two syringes containing atropine and pralodoxime chloride to counteract exposure to organophosphate nerve agents.

Narcosis - A state of deep unconsciousness caused by the influence of a drug or other chemical.

Narcotic - an agent that produces insensibility or stupor

National - Of a nationwide character, including the Federal, State, local, and tribal aspects of governance and polity.

National Disaster Medical System - A cooperative, asset-sharing partnership between the Department of Health and Human Services, the Department of Veterans Affairs, the Department of Homeland Security, and the Department of Defense. NDMS provides resources for meeting the continuity of care and mental health services requirements of the Emergency Support Function 8 in the Federal Response Plan.

National Incident Management System (NIMS) - A system mandated by HSPD-5 that provides a consistent nationwide approach for Federal, State, local, and tribal governments; the private sector; and nongovernmental organizations to work effectively and efficiently together to prepare for, respond to, and recover from domestic incidents, regardless of cause, size, or complexity. To provide for interoperability and compatibility among Federal, State, local, and tribal capabilities, the NIMS includes a core set of concepts, principles, and terminology. HSPD-5 identifies these as the ICS; multiagency coordination systems; training; identification and management of resources (including systems for classifying types of resources); qualification and certification; and the collection, tracking, and reporting of incident information and incident resources.

National Response Plan - A plan mandated by HSPD-5 that integrates Federal domestic prevention, preparedness, response, and recovery plans into one all-discipline, all-hazards plan.

National Toxicology Program (NTP) - Publishes "Annual Report on Carcinogens," listing substances either known or anticipated to be carcinogens.

NATO - North Atlantic Treaty Organization

NBC - Nuclear, Biological, or Chemical

NBC/M - NBC Weapons and Their Means of Delivery

NBCRS - NBC Reconnaissance System

NCO - Noncommissioned Officer

NCOIC - Noncommissioned Officer-in-Charge

NDAA - National Defense Authorization Act

NDMS - National Disaster Medical System

Necrosis - Cell or tissue death due to disease or injury. Death of tissue, usually as individual cells, group of cells, or in localized areas.

Necrotic - Pertaining to necrosis, end result of necrosis, dead.

Nephrotoxin - A chemical that causes kidney damage (e.g., uranium).

Nematicide - A pesticide used to control nematodes.

Nephrotoxins - Toxins that affect the urinary tract (kidneys, bladder, etc.).

Nerve Agent - Organic esters of phosphoric acid used as a chemical warfare agent because of their extreme toxicity (Tabun-GA, Sarin-GB, Soman-GD, GF, and VX). All are potent inhibitors of the enzyme, acetylcholinesterase, which is responsible for the degradation of the neurotransmitter, acetylcholine. Symptoms result from excess accumulation of acetylcholine in neuronal synapses or myoneural junctions. Nerve agents are readily absorbed by inhalation and/or through intact skin.

Neural - pertaining to a nerve or to the nerves

Neuropathy - functional disturbances and/or pathological changes in the peripheral nervous system

Neurotoxicity - exerting a destructive or poisonous effect on nerve tissue

Neurotoxins - A chemical whose primary toxic effect is on the nervous system (e.g., carbon disulfide).

Neutralization - Reaction of an acid and a base to form a salt. Reaction can be violent, may produce water (steam), heat or a gas. Altering the chemical, physical, and toxicological properties to render the chemical ineffective for use as intended.

Neutron Radiation – These neutrons are emitted from highly excited fission products. The way that neutrons interact with matter is quite different from the way that gamma rays interact. Neutrons have negligible interaction with atomic electrons. Neutron interaction in the human body can produce ionizing radiation and subsequent doses of radiation.

NFPA - An acronym for National Fire Protection Association, Inc.

NGO - Nongovernmental Organization

NIMS - National Incident Management System

NIOSH - National Institute for Occupational Safety and Health

NIS - New Independent States

Nitrogen Mustard - A form of blister agent that includes HN-1, HN-2, and HN-3.

NMD - National Missile Defense

No-Observed Adverse Effects Level (NOAEL) - An exposure level at which there are no statistically or biologically significant increases in the frequency or severity of adverse effects (to tissue, cells, organs, etc.) between the exposed population and its appropriate control (some effects may be produced at this level, but they are not considered as adverse, nor precursors to specific adverse effects). It is based on the highest exposure without adverse effect.

No-Observed Effects Level (NOEL) - An exposure level at which there are no statistically or biologically significant increases in the frequency or severity of any effect (to tissue, cells, organs, etc.) between the exposed population and its appropriate control.

Nocturia - excessive urination at night

Non-organic - Pesticides that do not contain organic molecules.

Non-persistent - Does not last long. Has become a very important term in reference to pesticides

Non-Pressure Tank Car - A tank car designed to transport products with an operating pressure of less than 100 psi. Normal operating pressure is atmospheric pressure or the vapor pressure of the product being transported.

Non selective - A pesticide that has an action against many species of pests rather than just a few.

No- target - Animals or plants within a pesticide treated area that are not intended to be controlled by the pesticide application.

Non-flammable - Not capable of being burned under normal conditions.

Nongovernmental Organization - An entity with an association that is based on interests of its members, individuals, or institutions and that is not created by a government, but may work cooperatively with government. Such organizations serve a public purpose, not a private benefit. Examples of NGOs include faith-based charity organizations and the American Red Cross.

Nonionic - Pertaining to an adjuvant that dissolves in the spray solution to produce no positive or negative ions.

Novichok agents In the late 1980s and early 1990s, Russia apparently produced several new agents that were made of chemicals not controlled by the Chemical Weapons Convention. In late 1992, a Russian chemist, Vil Mirzayanov, stated that a military research institute in Moscow had developed a new binary nerve agent more potent than VX called "novichok." He was subsequently arrested by the Russian Security Service for disclosing state secrets. The status of this research is unknown. Novichok is Russian for "newcomer."

Noxious - Something that is harmful to living organisms, such as noxious weeds.

NPT - Nuclear Non-Proliferation Treaty

NRP - National Response Plan

NSG - Nuclear Suppliers Group

Nuclear Radiation - Particulate and electromagnetic radiation emitted from atomic nuclei in various nuclear processes. The important nuclear radiations, from the weapons standpoint, are alpha and beta particles, gamma rays, and neutrons. All nuclear radiations are ionizing radiations, but the reverse is not true; X rays, for example, are included among ionizing radiations, but they are not nuclear radiations since they do not originate from atomic nuclei.

O

o- An abbreviation for "ortho". Referring to a particular arrangement of elements within a chemical molecule.

Ocular - pertaining to or affecting the eye

Odor Threshold - The lowest concentration of a material's vapor (or a gas) in air that is detectable by odor.

Officer - The ICS title for the personnel responsible for the Command Staff positions of Safety, Liaison, and Public Information.

OIC - Officer-in-Charge

Oleum - High strength sulfuric acid (> 100%). 100% sulfuric acid – Sulfur trioxide is added to increase the strength.

Olfactory - Refers to the sense of smell.

Oliguria - secretion of a diminished amount of urine in relation to fluid intake

Operational Period - The period of time scheduled for execution of a given set of operation actions as specified in the Incident Action Plan. Operational Periods can be of various lengths, although usually not over 24 hours.

Operations Level Trained - First responders at the operational level are those persons who respond to releases or potential releases of hazardous materials as part of the initial response to the incident for the purpose of protecting nearby persons, the environment, or property from the effects of the release. They shall be trained to respond in a defensive fashion to control the release from a safe distance and keep it from spreading. (ANSI/NFPA 472)

Operations Section - The Section responsible for all tactical operations at the incident. Includes Branches, Divisions and/or Groups, Task Forces, Strike Teams, Single Resources, and Staging Areas.

Ophthalmic - pertaining to the eye

Oral - Through the mouth - this is one of the routes of entry of pesticides into the body.

Oral Toxicity - The poisonous effects of a product when ingested (swallowed).

Organic Compounds - Chemical compounds which contain carbon. Examples are hydrocarbons and aromatic hydrocarbons. Volatile organic compounds vaporize at room temperature and pressure. They are found in many indoor sources, including many common household products and building materials.

Organic peroxide - A type of oxidizer that is very useful because of its reactive properties, considered by law (OSHA) to be a physical hazard.

Organochlorine - A class of pesticides, commonly used as insecticides, that contain a chlorine atom incorporated into an organic molecule. Organochlorines are often highly persistent. Many Organochlorine compounds are no longer used as pesticides.

Organophosphate - A commonly used class of pesticides; organophosphates are organic molecules containing phosphorus. Some organophosphates are highly toxic to people. Most break down in the environment very rapidly.

ORM - Means Other Regulated Material. Used in shipping descriptions.

Ornamentals - Usually refers to desirable plants.

OSCE - Organization for Security and Cooperation in Europe

OSD - Office of the Secretary of Defense

OSHA - Occupational Safety & Health Administration

OSIA - On Site Inspection Agency

Osteosclerosis - hardening or abnormal density of bone

Outage - The amount by which a package falls short of being liquid full. Usually expressed as a percent of volume or in inches.

Out-of-Service Resources - Resources assigned to an incident but unable to respond for mechanical, rest, or personnel reasons.

Overpressure - The transient pressure, usually expressed in pound per square inch, exceeding the ambient pressure, manifested in the shock wave from an explosion. The peak overpressure is the maximum value of the overpressure at a given location and is generally experienced at the instant the shock wave reaches that location.

Oxidation - A reaction in which a substance combines with oxygen to cause chemical change (e.g., fire). In a broader sense, oxidation is a reaction in which electrons are lost and is accompanied by reduction—a reaction in which electrons are gained.

Oxidizer - A chemical which supplies its own oxygen and which helps other combustible material burn more readily. A chemical which when mixed with combustible or flammable material will start a fire or make an existing fire worse. DOT defines oxidizer as a substance that yields oxygen readily to stimulate combustion.

Oxidizing Potential - the ability to give up oxygen or cause "oxidation" of organic and inorganic materials. The measure of a material to oxidize or lose electrons is known as its oxidation potential. Materials with a high Oxidizing Potential may effect measuring tools such as oxygen meters leading to false readings.

Oxidizing reagent - A chemical or substance that brings about oxidation.

Oxygen deficiency - An atmosphere having less than the normal percentage of oxygen found in normal air. Normal air contains 21% oxygen at sea level. Survivable levels of oxygen are down to 16%, but the standard references a 19.5% level that oxygen deficiency starts.

P

p- An abbreviation for "para". Referring to a particular arrangement of elements within a chemical molecule.

P - The letter "P" following a guide number in the yellow-bordered and blue-bordered pages identifies a material which may polymerize violently under high temperature conditions or contamination with other products. This polymerization will produce heat and high pressure buildup in containers which may explode or rupture.

Parasite - A plant or animal that lives upon or within another living organism at whose expense it obtains some advantage.

Pathway - A history of the flow of a pollutant from source to receptor, including qualitative descriptions of transport, medium, and exposure route.

P3I - Pre Planned Product Improvement

PAC - Patriot Advanced Capability

Packing group, PG - Grouping according to degree of danger presented by the hazardous material. Packing Group I represents the highest danger followed by Packing Group II, followed by Packing Group III.

Palpitation- unduly rapid heart beat which is noted by the patient; it may be regular or irregular

Parasite - A plant or animal that derives all its nutrients from another organism. Parasites often attach themselves to their host or invade the host's tissues. Parasitism may result in injury or death of the host.

Parasympathomimetic - producing effects resembling time of stimulation of the parasympathetic nerve supply to a part; called also cholinergic

Parenteral - not through the alimentary canal but rather by injection through some other route, such as subcutaneous, intramuscular, intravenous, etc.

Paresthesia- an abnormal sensation, as burning or prickling

Particle Size - The sizes of a particle, determined by the smallest dimension, for instance a diameter. It is usually expressed in micron measurements. Particles less than 50 microns cannot be seen without a microscope. Particles of 1-5 microns are the right size particle to settle in lower respiratory tract and get stuck. Any smaller and we exhale it, any larger and our bodies have some ability to filter it out or it settles on an environmental surfaces or gets stuck in the upper respiratory tract where it does not have as great an effect.

Pathogen - A microorganism that causes a disease.

PCO - Pest Control Operator

PDD - Presidential Decision Directive

PDS - Personnel Decontamination Station

PEL - Permissible Exposure Limit set by OSHA as a guide to acceptable levels of chemical exposure.

Pellet - A pesticide formulation consisting of the dry active ingredient and inert materials pressed into uniform sized granules.

Penetration - the act or process of piercing something. In protective clothing, it typically means passing through zippers, exhalation valves, or other potential openings that exist within the suit

Percent Volatile - The percentage of a chemical that will evaporate at ordinary temperatures. A high volatile percentage may mean there is more risk of explosion, or that dangerous fumes can be released. Evaporation rates are a better measure of the danger than the percent volatile measure.

Percutaneous - Denoting the passage of substances through unbroken skin, for example, by needle puncture, including introduction of wires and catheters.

Perennial - A plant that lives longer than two years - some may live indefinitely. Some perennial plants lose their leaves and become dormant during winter; others may die back and re-sprout from underground root structures each year. The evergreens are perennial plants that do not die back or become dormant.

Perfusion - liquid poured over or through an organ or tissue

Permeable - Allowing passage of fluids.

Permeated Contamination - Contamination which has either penetrated the surface or been absorbed into the material, making decontamination more difficult and labor intensive.

Permeation - to spread or flow throughout. In the case of protective clothing, it refers to a material's ability to be absorbed and passed into the interior of the clothing.

Permeation Rate - this average constant rate that occurs after breakthrough when the chemical contact is continuous and all forces affecting permeation have reached equilibrium.

Permissible Exposure Limit (PEL) - The Time Weighted Average (TWA) concentration at which 95% of exposed healthy adults will suffer no adverse effects over an 8-hour/day shift of a 40-hour work week. PELs are expressed in either ppm or mg/m3. PELs are enforceable by law, whereas TWAs are recommended limits.

Peroxide - Chemicals which contain two oxygen atoms bound together. Often explosive in nature. Could be shock or friction sensitive.

Persistence - Persistency is a contrived measurement of how long a chemical will remain in a liquid or solid form and thus remain a hazard

Persistent Agent - Chemical agents that do not hydrolyze or volatilize readily, such as VX and HD.

Personnel Accountability - The ability to account for the location and welfare of incident personnel. It is accomplished when supervisors ensure that ICS principles and processes are functional and that personnel are working within established incident management guidelines.

Pesticide - Any substance or mixture of substances intended for preventing, destroying, repelling, or mitigating any insects, rodents, nematodes, fungi, weeds, or any other forms of life declared to be pests; and any other substance or mixture of substances intended for use as a plant regulator, defoliant or desiccant.

Pesticide formulation - The pesticide as it comes from its original container, consisting of the active ingredient blended with inert materials.

Pesticide Resistance - Genetic qualities of a pest population that enable individuals to resist the effects of certain types of pesticides that are toxic to other members of that species.

PETN- Pentaerythritol tetranitrate- a high explosive frequently mixed with wax to make "Plastic Explosives" –also used as a treatment for angina in some heart patients.

PFP - Partnership for Peace

pH - A measure of the concentration of hydrogen ions in a solution - as the number of hydrogen ions increases, the solution becomes more acidic. The pH is a measure of how acidic or caustic a chemical is, based on a scale of 1 to 14. A pH of 1 means the chemical is very acidic. Pure water has a pH of 7. A pH of 14 means the chemical is very caustic. Both acidic and caustic substances are dangerous to skin and other valuable surfaces. A neutral level is expressed as a pH of 7.0. Designations above that level indicate increasing alkalinity, and designations below indicate increasing acidity. The pH is the accurate determination of the hydrogen ion concentration of a solution.

Pharynx - the muscular membrane sac between the mouth and nostrils and the esophagus

Pheromone - A chemical produced by an animal to attract other animals of the same species.

Phosgene - a colorless, heavier than air, chemical agent designed to cause pulmonary damage and asphyxia. The military designator for this agent is CG, and the similar and related chemical diphosgene is designated as DP. There have been a number of accidental fatalities involving phosgene exposure in chemical manufacture.

Phosgene oxime (CX) Dichloroformoxine is a powerful irritant which produces immediate reactions varying from a mild irritation to severe local pain. This agent is classified either as an urticariant or a blister agent depending on source

Photon - A unit or 'particle' of electromagnetic radiation, carrying a quantum of energy which is characteristic of that particular radiation.

Photophobia- abnormal visual intolerance of light

Photosensitize - to induce a state of abnormal responsiveness to the influence of light

Physical Change - phase change: a change from one state (solid or liquid or gas) to another without a change in chemical composition.

Physical Properties - those properties that do not involve a change in the chemical identity of the substance. They affect the physical behavior of the material inside and outside the container such as the change of the state of the material: boiling point, specific gravity, vapor density, and water solubility.

Physical State - the state in which a substance exists at a certain temperature and pressure ie solid, liquid or gas. Physical state is usually determined at Standard Temperature (70°F) and Standard Pressure (1 atmosphere).

Phytotoxic - Injurious (toxic) to plants. Poisonous to plants; inhibiting plant growth.

Picrates such as Lead Picrate- Salts of Picric acid (trinitrophenol) used as primary explosives and in ammunition.

PIH - Poison Inhalation Hazard. Term used to describe gases and volatile liquids that are toxic when inhaled.

PIO - Public Information Officer

Placard - A sign or symbol designed to be hung on a wall, container or vehicle containing warning information to convey the level of hazard.

Plague - An acute infectious disease caused by Yersinia pestis. Under normal conditions, humans become infected as a result of contact with rodents and their fleas. In a biological warfare scenario, the plague bacillus could be delivered by means of contaminated vectors (fleas) causing the bubonic type or, more likely, by means of aerosol causing the pneumonic type. The incubation period is 2 to 8 days following the bite of an infected flea and is characterized by high fever; chills;

prostration; enlarged, painful lymph nodes known as buboes, located particularly in the groin or under the arms. The bacteria can invade the blood stream leading to the septicemic form of the disease. Subsequent invasion of the lungs causes a rapidly fatal form known as pneumonic plague that can be transmitted from person-to-person via airborne respiratory droplets. The agent is highly infectious by the aerosol route and most populations are completely susceptible.

Planning Meeting - A meeting held as needed throughout the duration of an incident, to select specific strategies and tactics for incident control operations, and for service and support planning. On larger incidents, the Planning Meeting is a major element in the development of the Incident Action Plan (IAP).

Planning Section - Responsible for the collection, evaluation, and dissemination of information related to the incident, and for the preparation and documentation of Incident Action Plans. The Section also maintains information on the current and forecasted situation, and on the status of resources assigned to the incident. Includes the Situation, Resources, Documentation, and Demobilization Units, as well as Technical Specialists.

Plant Growth Regulator - A pesticide used to regulate or alter the normal growth of plants or development of plan parts.

Plume - Effluent cloud resulting from a continuous source release.

Pneumatic Hopper – A non-tank freight car that is unloaded by pressurizing the car body to remove the product. Generally used for very fine solids, dusts or powders.

Poison - A chemical that, in relatively small amounts, is able to produce injury by chemical action when it comes in contact with a susceptible tissue.

POLREP - Pollution Report

Polydipsia - excessive thirst persisting for long periods of time

Polymerase Chain Reaction (PCR) - An in-vitro method for enzymatically synthesizing and amplifying defined sequences of DNA in molecular biology. It can be used for improving DNA-based diagnostic procedures for identifying unknown biological warfare agents.

Polymerization - Describes what is often a violent reaction, involving the process of forming a compound from several single molecules of the same substance. In polymer chemistry, polymerization is a process of reacting monomer molecules together in a chemical reaction to form three-dimensional networks or polymer chains. There are many forms of polymerization and different systems exist to categorize them

Post-emergence or Post-emergent - An herbicide applied after emergence of a specified weed or crop.

Powder - A finely ground dust containing active ingredient and inert materials. This powder is mixed with water before application as a liquid spray.

ppb - Parts per billion. One ppb represents one microgram of something per liter of water (ug/l), or one microgram of something per kilogram of soil (ug/kg).

PPE - Personal Protective Equipment

ppm - Parts per million. One ppm is equivalent to 1 milligram of something per liter of water (mg/l) or 1 milligram of something per kilogram soil (mg/kg). For example: 1 percent equals 10,000 ppm.

PPQ - Plant Protection and Quarantine.

Pralidoxime Currently the United States Army uses pralidoxime chloride (2-PAM) to reactivate cholinesterase in the NAAK Mark I kits.

Pre-emergent - The action of an herbicide that controls specified weeds as they sprout from seeds before they push through the soil surface.

Precordial - pertaining to the region over the heart and lower part of the thorax

Preparedness - The range of deliberate, critical tasks and activities necessary to build, sustain, and improve the operational capability to prevent, protect against, respond to, and recover from domestic incidents. Preparedness is a continuous process. Preparedness involves efforts at all levels of government and between government and private-sector and nongovernmental organizations to identify threats, determine vulnerabilities, and identify required resources. Within the NIMS, preparedness is operationally focused on establishing guidelines, protocols, and standards for planning, training and exercises, personnel qualification and certification, equipment certification, and publication management.

Preparedness Organizations - The groups and forums that provide interagency coordination for domestic incident management activities in a nonemergency context. Preparedness organizations can include all agencies with a role in incident management, for prevention, preparedness, response, or recovery activities. They represent a wide variety of committees, planning groups, and other organizations that meet and coordinate to ensure the proper level of planning, training, equipping, and other preparedness requirements within a jurisdiction or area.

Pressure Tank Car. A tank car designed to operate with internal pressure in excess of 100 psi. from the pressure exerted by the product being transported.

Prevention - Actions to avoid an incident or to intervene to stop an incident from occurring. Prevention involves actions to protect lives and property. It involves applying intelligence and other information to a range of activities that may include such countermeasures as deterrence operations; heightened inspections; improved surveillance and security operations; investigations to determine the full nature and source of the threat; public health and agricultural surveillance and testing processes; immunizations, isolation, or quarantine; and, as appropriate, specific law enforcement operations aimed at deterring, preempting, interdicting, or disrupting illegal activity and apprehending potential perpetrators and bringing them to justice.

Private Sector - Organizations and entities that are not part of any governmental structure. It includes for-profit and not-for-profit organizations, formal and informal structures, commerce and industry, and private voluntary organizations (PVO).

Processes - Systems of operations that incorporate standardized procedures, methodologies, and functions necessary to provide resources effectively and efficiently. These include resource typing, resource ordering and tracking, and coordination.

Procurement Unit - Functional Unit within the Finance/Administration Section responsible for financial matters involving vendor contracts.

Properties - The characteristics by which a substance may be identified. Physical properties describe its state of matter, color, odor, and density; chemical properties describe its behavior in reaction with other materials.

Protection Factor - With PPE, it is the ratio of the concentration outside the protective equipment to the concentration inside the protective equipment. Measurement sites are critical for proper determination (e.g., for a protective mask, the measurements inside the mask would be made at a subject's breathing zone, and the measurements outside the mask would be made in a corresponding zone).

Protective clothing - Includes both respiratory and physical protection. One cannot assign a level of protection to clothing or respiratory devices separately. These levels were accepted and defined by response organizations such as U.S. Coast Guard, NIOSH, and U.S. EPA.

Proton - A particle of mass unity (approximately) carrying a unit positive charge; it is identical physically with the nucleus of the ordinary hydrogen atom. All atomic nuclei contain protons.

Proteinuria- an excess of serum proteins in the urine; also called albuminuria

Pruritis - Itching.

PS Chloropicrin—a lachrymator rarely used as a crowd control agent because of its toxicity and likelihood to cause fatalities.

PSI - Pounds per square inch. A measure of blast overpressure or dynamic pressure, used to calculate the effects of an explosion.

PSIA – Pounds per square inch absolute - The sum of gauge and atmospheric pressures, which will vary with altitude.

PSIG – Pounds per Square Inch Gauge - Fluid pressure (liquid and gas) as measured on a pressure gauge without the inclusion of atmospheric pressure.

Psychosis - any major mental disorder characterized by derangement of the personality and loss of contact with reality

Psychotropic - exerting an effect upon the mind; capable of modifying mental activity

Public Information Officer (PIO) - A member of the Command Staff responsible for interfacing with the public and media or with other agencies with incident-related information requirements.

Publications Management - The publications management subsystem includes materials development, publication control, publication supply, and distribution. The development and distribution of NIMS materials is managed through this subsystem. Consistent documentation is critical to success, because it ensures that all responders are familiar with the documentation used in a particular incident regardless of the location or the responding agencies involved.

Pulmonary - pertaining to the lungs

Pulmonary edema - Fluid in the lungs; associated with an outpouring of fluids from the capillaries into the pulmonary spaces (air sacs or alveoli) producing severe shortness of breath. In later stages, produces expectoration of frothy, pink, serious fluid and cyanosis.

Pungent - Sharp or irritating odor.

Pupa - In insects having complete metamorphosis, the resting life stage between larval and adult forms.

PVO - Private Voluntary Organizations

Pyrethroid - A synthetic pesticide that mimics pyrethrin, a botanical pesticide derived from certain species of chrysanthemum flowers.

Pyrophoric - A chemical that can ignite spontaneously in air at or below 130°F.

Q

QDR - Quadrennial Defense Review

Q Fever - An acute, febrile, incapacitating disease caused by the rickettsial bacterium Coxiella burnetti and transmitted via inhalation of contaminated aerosols, the bites of infected ticks or ingestion of milk from infected dairy animals. A biological warfare attack would cause diseasesimilar to that occurring naturally.

Qualification and Certification - This subsystem provides recommended qualification and certification standards for emergency responder and incident management personnel. It also allows the development of minimum standards for resources expected to have an interstate application. Standards typically include training, currency, experience, and physical and medical fitness.

R

R&D - Research and Development

RAD - Radiation Absorbed Dose

Radiation - Usually refers to the radiant energy emitted by certain elements (such as radium, uranium, plutonium, thorium, and their products). Radiation is often in the form of alpha particles, beta particles, or gamma rays.

Radiation Sickness - The complex of symptoms characterizing the disease known as radiation injury, resulting from excessive exposure of the whole body (or large part) to ionizing radiation. The earliest of these symptoms is nausea, fatigue, vomiting, and diarrhea, which may be followed by loss of hair, hemorrhage, inflammation of the mouth and throat, and general loss of energy. In severe cases, where the radiation has been approximately 1,000 rad or more, death may occur within two to four weeks. Those who survive six weeks after the receipt of a single large dose of radiation to the whole body may generally be expected to recover.

Radioactivity - Describes the spontaneous emission of particles or rays from substances that are called radioactive elements. Generally alpha or beta particles, often accompanied by gamma rays, from the nuclei of an unstable isotope. As a result of this emission the radioactive isotope is converted (or decays) into the isotope of a different (daughter) element which may or may not be unstable. Ultimately, as a result of one or more stages of radioactive decay, a stable (nonradioactive) end product is formed

Rail Burns - Deformations of the tank shell caused by the tank passing over a stationary object. Rail burns most often contain a dent and a gouge at the bottom of the dent. Rail burns can be large and may cross weld seam.

Rales- abnormal respiratory sound heard when listening for sounds within the body

Rate – In pesticide application, the quantity or volume of liquid spray, dust or granules that is applied to an area over a specified period of time.

RCRA - The Resource Conservation and Recovery Act (of 1976). A Federal statute which establishes a framework for proper management and disposal of all wastes. Generation, transportation, storage, treatment, and disposal of hazardous wastes are all regulated under this Act.

RDX also called hexogen, cyclonite, cyclotromethylene, trinitramine, Research Department Explosive, and Royal Demolition Explosive. Used in Plastic Explosives for legitimate and terrorist purposes. Cyclotrimethylenetrinitramine

Reactivity - Reactivity refers to the rate at which a chemical substance tends to undergo a chemical reaction in time. In pure compounds, reactivity is regulated by the physical properties of the sample. For instance, grinding a sample to a higher specific surface area increases its reactivity. A substance's susceptibility to undergoing a chemical reaction or change that may
result in dangerous side effects, such as explosions, burning, and corrosive or toxic emissions. The conditions that cause the reaction, such as heat, other chemicals, and being dropped, will usually be specified as "Conditions to Avoid" when a chemical's reactivity is discussed on an MSDS.

Reception Area - This refers to a location separate from staging areas, where resources report in for processing and out-processing. Reception Areas provide accountability, security, situational awareness briefings, safety awareness, distribution of IAPs, supplies and equipment, feeding, and bed down.

Recommended Exposure Limit (REL) - The time weighted average (TWA) concentration that should not be exceeded during a ten hour work day during a 40 hour week.

Recorders - Individuals within ICS organizational units who are responsible for recording information. Recorders may be found in Planning, Logistics, and Finance/Administration Units.

Recovery - The development, coordination, and execution of service- and site-restoration plans; the reconstitution of government operations and services; individual, private-sector, nongovernmental, and public-assistance programs to provide housing and to promote restoration; long-term care and treatment of affected persons; additional measures for social, political, environmental, and economic restoration; evaluation of the incident to identify lessons learned; Post-incident reporting; and development of initiatives to mitigate the effects of future incidents.

Recovery Plan - A plan developed by a State, local, or tribal jurisdiction with assistance from responding Federal agencies to restore the affected area.

Recumbent - lying down

Refrigerated liquid - See "Cryogenic liquid".

Reinforced Response - Those resources requested in addition to the initial response.

REL – Recommended Exposure Limits – NIOSH

Relief Valve - A valve usually held closed by a spring and which is forced open when pressure in the vessel to which it is attached rises above a predetermined level. Spring loaded valves are designed to re-close when the internal pressure falls below the set pressure of the spring. Often called a safety relief valve, safety relief device or pressure relief valve.

REM - A unit of biological dose of radiation; the name is derived from the initial letters of the term "roentgen equivalent man (or mammal)." The number of rems of radiation is equal to the number of rads absorbed multiplied by the RBE of the given radiation (for a specified effect).

- The rem is also the unit of dose equivalent, which is equal to the product of the number of rads absorbed and the "quality factor" of the radiation

Renal- pertaining to the kidney

Repellent - A pesticide used to keep target pests away from a treated area by saturating the area with an odor that is disagreeable to the pest.

Reporting Locations - Location or facilities where incoming resources can check in at the incident. (See Check-in.)

Reporting Marks - A unique set of initials and numbers assigned to a railroad car or locomotive. They are stenciled to freight cars on both sides and on both ends. The reporting marks are crucial for obtaining information about the contents of that particular car as they are unique to each car.

Reproductive toxins - Chemicals that affect the reproductive capabilities, including chromosomal damage (mutations) and effects on fetuses (teratogenesis).

Reproductive Effect - A toxic effect of a substance that is evident in the second or third generation of exposed grandparents.

Residue - Material remaining in a package after unloading.

Resistance - The physical or chemical ability of certain organisms to neutralize the effects of certain compounds.

Resource Management - Efficient incident management requires a system for identifying available resources at all jurisdictional levels to enable timely and unimpeded access to resources needed to prepare for, respond to, or recover from an incident. Resource management under the NIMS includes mutual-aid agreements; the use of special Federal, State, local, and tribal teams; and resource mobilization protocols.

Resources - Personnel and major items of equipment, supplies, and facilities available or potentially available for assignment to incident operations and for which status is maintained. Resources are described by kind and type and may be used in operational support or supervisory capacities at an incident or at an EOC.

Resources Unit - Functional unit within the Planning Section responsible for recording the status of resources committed to the incident. This unit also evaluates resources currently committed to the incident, the effects additional responding resources will have on the incident, and anticipated resource needs.

Response - Activities that address the short-term, direct effects of an incident. Response includes immediate actions to save lives, protect property, and meet basic human needs. Response also includes the execution of emergency operations plans and of mitigation activities designed to limit the loss of life, personal injury, property damage, and other unfavorable outcomes. As indicated by the situation, response activities include applying intelligence and other information to lessen the effects or consequences of an incident; increased security operations; continuing investigations into nature and source of the threat; ongoing public health and agricultural surveillance and testing processes; immunizations, isolation, or quarantine; and specific law enforcement operations aimed at preempting, interdicting, or disrupting illegal activity, and apprehending actual perpetrators and bringing them to justice.

Response - That portion of incident management in which personnel are involved in controlling a hazardous materials incident. (ANSI/NFPA 471)

RESTAT - Resources Status

Restricted Use - Any compound for which a special license or permit is required before it can be purchased or used.

Rhinitis - Inflammation of nasal mucous.

Rhinorrhea - Thin watery discharge from the nose; runny nose.

Ricin - A glycoprotein toxin from the seed of the castor plant. It blocks protein synthesis by altering the RNA, thus killing the cell. Ricin's significance as a potential biological warfare agent relates to its availability worldwide, ease of production, and extreme pulmonary toxicity when inhaled.

Rickettsia - A microorganism of the genus Rickettisia, made up of small rod-shaped coccoids occurring intracytoplasmically or free in the lumen of the gut of lice, fleas, ticks, and mites, by which they are transmitted to man and other animals. They cause diseases such as typhus, scrub typhus, and Rocky Mountain Spotted Fever in humans.

Rift Valley Fever - One of the viral hemorrhagic fevers caused by the Bunyaviridae viral group. It is transmitted to humans by Aedes Aegypti mosquitoes. It may affect the retina of the eye, leading to permanent blindness.

Riot Control Agents - Compounds widely used by governments for domestic law enforcement purposes and which produce transient effects on man that disappear within minutes after removal from exposure.

Risk - A measure of the chances that damage to life, property, or the environment will occur if a hazard occurs. Risk includes consideration of the severity of the damage.

Risk Assessment - Broadly defined as the scientific activity of evaluating the toxic properties of a chemical and the conditions of human exposure to it, with the objective of determining the probability that exposed humans will be adversely affected. Its four main components are:
1. Hazard Identification—Does the agent cause the effect?
2. Dose-Response Assessment—What is the relationship between the dose and its incidence in human beings?
3. Exposure Assessment—What exposures are experienced or anticipated, and under what conditions?
4. Risk Characterization—The total analysis producing an estimate of the incidence of the adverse effect in a given population.

Risk Management - A decision-making process that entails consideration of political, social, economic, and engineering information with risk-assessment information to develop, analyze, and compare regulatory options and to select the appropriate regulatory response to a potential health risk.

Rocky Mountain spotted fever- a rickettsial disease characterized by sudden onset of fever, severe headache, fatigue, swollen and redden eyes, muscle pain, and chills. About 25% of untreated cases are fatal.

Rodenticide - A pesticide used for control of rats, mice, gophers, squirrels and other rodents.

Roentgen - A unit of exposure to gamma (or X) radiation. It is defined precisely as the quantity of gamma (or X) rays that will produce electrons (in ion pairs) with a total charge of 2.58 x 10-4 coulomb in 1 kilogram of dry air. An exposure of 1 roentgen results in the deposition of about 94 ergs of energy in 1 gram of soft body tissue. Hence, an exposure of 1 roentgen is approximately equivalent to an absorbed dose of 1 rad in soft tissue.

RP Red Phosphorus---burning RP causes the formation of toxic phosphorus smoke which can severely damage the lungs and mucous membranes

Running Gear - A general term used to describe the group of parts whose functions are related to the movement of the car. Running Gear includes the wheels, axles, bearings, suspension systems and the trucks.

ROSS - Resource Ordering and Status System

Routes of exposure –
- Inhalation: Irritants or toxins enter the body through the nose, mouth, and lungs as a result of the respiratory process.
- Ingestion: The process of consuming contaminated food or water.
- Absorption: The process by which hazardous materials are absorbed into the body through the skin.
- Injection: The process by which a toxic substance is introduced directly into the blood bya needle, cannula or some other mechanical means.

RQ - Reportable quantity of a hazardous substance.

RSCAAL - Remote Sensing Chemical Agent Alarm

Runoff - Excess water produced during firefighting or from rain. Water from rain, snow melt, or irrigation that flows over the ground surface and returns to streams.

S

SA—Military designation for Arsine (AsH3) which is a true blood agent.

Safety Officer - A member of the Command Staff responsible for monitoring and assessing safety hazards or unsafe situations and for developing measures for ensuring personnel safety. The Safety Officer may have Assistants.

Safety Appliances - Any one of several specific components required on rail cars, the function of which is directly related to the safety of train crew members and other persons who are on or around the rail equipment. They include hand brakes, ladders, and sill steps, uncoupling levers.

Safety Vent - A term applied to devices designed to allow excess internal pressure to be released from a tank car. A safety vent usually includes a single use device like a rupture disk that breaks at a set pressure. Safety vents are usually one-time use devices and allow the product to be open to the atmosphere until replaced or repaired.

SALAD - Shipboard Automatic Liquid Agent Detector

Salmonella - A group of nonspore forming bacteria capable of causing gastroenteritis, enteric fever, bactermia, and localized infections. After ingestion of contaminated food or water, nausea,vomiting, diarrhea, fever headache, and muscle aches will occur lasting between 2 to 7 days.

SARA Title III - Superfund Amendments and Reauthorization Act of 1986. Title III of SARA, the Emergency Planning and Community Right-to-Know Act of 1986, includes detailed provisions for community planning.

Sarin - Isopropyl methylphosphonofluoridate; it is a non-persistent organophosphate nerve agentalso known as GB. Its chemical formula is C4H10FO2P.

Saturated Hydrocarbon – a hydrocarbon containing only carbon and hydrogen. Alkanes, alsoknown as paraffins, are chemical compounds that consist only of the elements carbon (C) and hydrogen (H) (i.e., hydrocarbons), wherein these atoms are linked together exclusively by single bonds (i.e., they are saturated compounds) without any cyclic structure (i.e. loops).

SAW - Surface Acoustic Wave—a form of chemical agent monitor no longer used due to its relative insensitivity to the presence of contaminants at dangerous levels.

Saxitoxin - The parent compound of a family of chemically related neurotoxins. In nature they are predominantly produced by marine dinoflagellates, although they have also been identified in association with such diverse organisms as blue-green algae, crabs, and the blue-ringed octopus. The natural route of exposure to these toxins is oral. In a biological warfare scenario, the most likely route of delivery would be by inhalation or toxic projectile. It could also be used in a confined area to contaminate water supplies.

SBIRS - Space Based Infrared System

SCBA - An acronym for Self-Contained Breathing Apparatus. SCBA includes a seal tested mask, positive pressure regulator and a pressurized air supply.

Scores - Indentations in the tank caused by a blunt object coming in contact with the tank. A score is characterized by the relocation of the tank or weld metal so that the metal is pushed aside, reducing the thickness of the tank shell.

Scotoma - an area of depressed vision within the visual field, surrounded by an area of less depressed or normal vision

SDK - Skin Decontamination Kit

SDO - Standards Development Organizations

sec - An abbreviation for "secondary". Referring to a particular arrangement of elements within a chemical molecule.

Secondary Contamination - Contaminants can be carried away from the immediate release areaand have serious health consequences beyond the scene of the emergency.

Section - The organizational level having responsibility for a major functional area of incident management, e.g., Operations, Planning, Logistics, Finance/Administration, and Intelligence (if established). The section is organizationally situated between the branch and the Incident Command.

Segment - A geographical area in which a Task Force/Strike Team Leader or Supervisor of a single resource is assigned authority and responsibility for the coordination of resources and implementation of planned tactics. A segment may be a portion of a division or an area inside or outside the perimeter of an incident. Segments are identified with Arabic numbers (1,2,3,4-etc.).

Selective Pesticide - A pesticide that has a mode of action against only a single or small number of pest species.

Self-accelerating decomposition temperature (SADT) - Temperature above which the decomposition of an unstable substance continues unimpeded, regardless of the ambient or external temperature. SADT means the lowest temperature at which self-accelerating decomposition may occur for a substance in the packaging as used in transport.

Self-Contained Breathing Apparatus (SCBA) – Type of respiratory protection. Consists of a harness, bottle, regulator and face piece. Highest level of respiratory protection.

Sensitizer - a substance which on first exposure causes little or no reaction in humans or test animals but which on repeated exposure may cause a marked response not necessarily limited to the contact site. Skin sensitization is the most common form of sensitization in the industrial setting, although respiratory sensitization to a few chemicals is also known to occur.

Sensitizer/allergen – A chemical that causes a substantial proportion of exposed people or animals to develop an allergic reaction in normal tissue after repeated exposure to the chemicals

SERC - State Emergency Response Commission.

Service Branch - A Branch within the Logistics Section responsible for service activities at the incident. Includes the Communication, Medical, and Food Units.

Service Container - Any container designed to hold concentrate or diluted pesticide mixtures, including the sprayer tank, but not the original pesticide container.

Shelter in Place - Protect people without evacuating by keeping them inside a building with windows and doors closed and external ventilation systems shut off until a hazardous situation has resolved.

Short-line railroad (also Short Line) Independent railway companies operating over relatively short distances.

Sievert (Sv) - The modern unit of radiation does, incorporating quality factors for the biological effectiveness of different types of ionizing radiation (implying that alpha particles are 20 times more dangerous than X-rays depositing the same amount of energy in tissues).

Signal Word - The word "Danger", "Warning", or "Caution" that appears on a pesticide label that signifies how toxic the pesticide is and what toxicity category it belongs to.

Simple Asphyxiant - Generally, an inert gas that displaces the oxygen necessary for breathing, and dilutes the oxygen concentration below the level that is useful for the human body.

Single Resource - An individual, a piece of equipment and its personnel complement, or a crew or team of individuals with an identified work Supervisor that can be used on an incident.

Site - The area which can be treated with certain chemicals.

SITREP - Situation Report

Situation Unit - Functional Unit within the Planning Section responsible for the collection, organization, and analysis of incident status information, and for analysis of the situation as it progresses. Reports to the Planning Section Chief.

Sizeup - The rapid mental evaluation of the factors that influence an incident. Sizeup is the first step in determining a course of action

SLBM - Submarine Launched Ballistic Missile

Slurry - A suspension of insoluble particles (as plaster of Paris or lime or clay etc.) usually in water. A slurry is, in general, a thick suspension of solids in a liquid.

SLV - Space Launch Vehicle

Smallpox - An acute, systemic, potentially fatal and highly contagious viral disease caused by the variola Orthopoxvirus; characterized by the appearance of skin lesions and pustules on the face and body, with chills and fever. Under natural conditions, the virus is transmitted by direct (face-to-face) contact with an infected case, by fomites, and occasionally by aerosols.

SO - Safety Officer

Solubility - The degree to which one material may be completely mixed with or dissolved in another material. Solubility is the property of a solid, liquid, or gaseous chemical substance called solute to dissolve in a liquid solvent to form a homogeneous solution. The solubility of a substance strongly depends on the used solvent as well as on temperature and pressure.

Soluble - Material dissolves in water or other stated material.

Solubility in Water - An indicator of the amount of a chemical that can be dissolved in water, shown as a percentage or as a description. A low percent of solubility (or a description of "slight" solubility or "low" solubility) means that only a small amount will dissolve in water. Knowing this may help firefighters or personnel cleaning a spill.

Soluble Powder - A pesticide formulation where the active ingredient and all inert ingredients completely dissolve in water to form a true solution.

Solute - Material that is dissolved in a solvent.

Solution - Homogenous liquid mixture of two or more chemical compounds or elements that will not undergo any segregation under normal conditions. A liquid that contains dissolved substances, such as a soluble pesticide.

Solvent - A liquid capable of dissolving certain chemicals.

Soman - The chemical Pinacolyl methyl phosphonofluoridate, methyl-1, 2, 2-trimethylpropyl ester. It is a nerve agent known as GD; its chemical formula is $(CH_3)_3CCH(CH_3)OPF(O)CH_3$.

SOP - Standard Operating Procedure

Span of Control - The number of individuals a supervisor is responsible for, usually expressed as the ratio of supervisors to individuals. (Under the NIMS, an appropriate span of control is between 1 -3 and 1 -7.)

Specific gravity - Ratio of the weight of a volume of liquid or solid to the weight of an equal volume of water (the specific gravity of water is, therefore, 1.0). A substance with a specific gravity greater than 1.0 will sink in water; whereas one with a specific gravity less than 1.0 will float on water. Most flammable liquids are lighter than water.

Spontaneous combustion - Process where heat is generated within a material by slow oxidation until combustion takes place.

Spot Treatment - Directed at specified or limited area instead of a general overall application; spot not to exceed 2 sq. feet, but may be next to each other with space left between each spot.

Spreader - An adjuvant that lowers the surface tension of treated surfaces to enable the pesticide to be absorbed.

SRBM - Short Range Ballistic Missile (Range - 1,000 kilometers or less)

Stabilized - Containing a small amount of another substance included to keep the first material from changing form.

Staphylococcus Enterotoxin Type B (SEB) - An incapacitating toxin produced by the bacterium Staphylococcus aureus; responsible for the fever, chills, and gastrointestinal upsets of "food poisoning" from ingestion of improperly prepared food items. The weaponized form is an aerosol; potent incapacitator in small doses; could render up to 80 percent of exposed personnel clinically ill for approximately two weeks. A rapid acting toxin that causes vomiting, diarrhea, and painful cramps.

Staging Area - Location established where resources can be placed while awaiting a tactical assignment. The Operations Section manages Staging Areas.

START - Strategic Arms Reduction Treaty

State - When capitalized, refers to any State of the United States, the District of Columbia, the Commonwealth of Puerto Rico, the Virgin Islands, Guam, American Samoa, the Commonwealth of the Northern Mariana Islands, and any possession of the United States. See Section 2 (14), Homeland Security Act of 2002, Pub. L. 107-296, 116 Stat. 2135 (2002).

STB - Super Topical Bleach   High strength bleach solution

STCC Identification Numbers - An acronym for Standard Transportation Commodity Code. A seven digit identification number commonly used for materials shipped by rail. Numbers beginning with 49- are hazardous materials.

STEL - Short term exposure limit

Straight (solid) stream - Method used to apply or distribute water from the end of a hose. The water is delivered under pressure for penetration. In an efficient straight (solid) stream, approximately 90% of the water passes through an imaginary circle 38 cm (15 inches) in diameter at the breaking point. Hose (solid or straight) streams are frequently used to cool tanks and other equipment exposed to flammable liquid fires, or for washing burning spills away from danger points. However, straight streams will cause a spill fire to spread if improperly used or when directed into open containers of flammable and combustible liquids. (See also water spray)

Strategic - Strategic elements of incident management are characterized by continuous long-term, high-level planning by organizations headed by elected or other senior officials. These elements involve the adoption of long-range goals and objectives, the setting of priorities; the establishment of budgets and other fiscal decisions, policy development, and the application of measures of performance or effectiveness.

Strategy - The general direction selected to accomplish incident objectives set by the Incident Commander.

Strength - A term used to described the concentration of a solution. The strength of an acid refers to its ability or tendency to lose a proton. A strong acid is one that completely dissociates in water.

Strike Team - A specified combination of the same kind and type of resources with common communications and a Leader.

Stub Sill - A short longitudinal structural member of a car underframe designed to accommodate the coupler and draft gear, and to transmit coupler forces to the car body on cars with no through center sill. Common stub sill applications are found on tank cars and covered hoppers.

Structural Pest - Pest which will attack structures or buildings and destroy or damage them.

Sublimation - Passing of a substance directly from the solid state to the vapor state without passing through the liquid state. Solids such as naphthalene (moth balls) are an example.

Sublime - To change from a solid state to a gaseous state without becoming a liquid.

Subsidiary hazard - Means hazard of a material other than the primary hazard.

Sulfur Mustard - A blister agent also known as H (or HD) for distilled mustard. Bis(2-chloroethyl) sulfide. The chemical formula is C4H8Cl2S.

Supertropical Bleach - bleaching agent containing calcium hypochlorite (a powerful oxidizer) and calcium oxide (a corrosive material)

Supervisor - The ICS title for individuals responsible for a Division or Group.

Supply Unit - Functional Unit within the Support Branch of the Logistics Section responsible for ordering equipment and supplies required for incident operations.

Support Branch - A Branch within the Logistics Section responsible for providing personnel, equipment, and supplies to support incident operations. Includes the Supply, Facilities, and Ground Support Units.

Support Resources - Nontactical resources under the supervision of the Logistics, Planning, Finance/Administration Sections, or the Command Staff.

Supporting Materials - Refers to the several attachments that may be included with an Incident Action Plan, e.g., communications plan, map, safety plan, traffic plan, and medical plan.

Supporting Technologies - Any technology that may be used to support the NIMS is included in this subsystem. These technologies include orthophoto mapping, remote automatic weather stations, infrared technology, and communications, among various others.

Surface contamination - Contamination which remains on top of a material making it accessible to the decontaminant and easily removed or neutralized.

Surface tension - Describes the attractive force between the surface molecules of a liquid.

Surfactant - A compound which reduces the surface tension of water for better spreading and sticking.

Susceptible - Easily affected by.

Swift Water Search and Rescue Team (Flood Search and Rescue; Water Rescue Team) Team conducts surface search and rescue operations on waterways where the water is moving fast enough to produce sufficient force to present a life and safety hazard to a person entering it.

Synonym - Another name by which a chemical is known. For example, synonyms for methyl alcohol are methanol and wood alcohol.

Symptom - Information related by an individual about himself/herself that may indicate illness or injury. Signs or observations are made about an individual or an animal that may indicate illness or injury.

Synergism - A reaction in which a chemical that has no pesticidal qualities can enhance the toxicity of a pesticide it is mixed with.

Synergistic Effect - A biological response to exposure to multiple chemicals which is greater than the sum of the effects of the individual agents.

sym - An abbreviation for "symmetrical". Referring to a particular arrangement of elements within a chemical molecule.

Synergy - An interaction of materials or chemicals to give a result different from either material or chemical alone. Usually thought of as two materials reacting to give a third material that is potentially more dangerous than either of the first materials.

Systemic - pertaining to or affecting the body or organism as a whole. Spread throughout the body, affecting all body symptoms and organs, not localized in one spot or area.

Systemic Effects - Effects that require absorption and distribution of the toxicant to a site distant from its portal of entry, at which point effects are produced. Most chemicals that produce systemic toxicity do not cause a similar degree of toxicity in all organs, but usually demonstrate major toxicity to one or two organs. These are referred to as target organs of toxicity for that chemical.

Systemic Pesticide - A pesticide that is taken up into the tissues of the organism and transported to other locations where it will affect pests.

Systemic poison - A substance that has a toxic effect upon several organ systems of the body.

Systemic Toxicants - Chemical compounds that affect entire organ systems, often operating far from the original site of entry.

T

t- - An abbreviation for "tertiary". Referring to a particular arrangement of elements within a chemical molecule.

T (upper case) - Bis[2-(2-chloroethylthio)ethyl] ether. The chemical formula is $C8H16Cl2OS2$. T is a sulfur, oxygen and chlorine compound similar in structure to HD. When T is added to HD, the resulting mixture has enhanced physiological and physical effects, making it a more effective chemical warfare agent.

T-2 Mycotoxin - A trichothecene mycotoxin produced by filamentous fungi growing on moldy cereal grains.

Tabun - Ethyl N,N-dimethylphosphoramidocyanidate. This is a non- persistent organophosphate nerve agent also known as GA. Its chemical formula is $C5H11N2O2P$.

Tachycardia - A rapid heart rate (over 90 beats per minute).

Tactical Direction - Direction given by the Operations Section Chief that includes the tactics required to implement the selected strategy, the selection and assignment of resources to carry out the tactics, directions for tactics implementation, and performance monitoring for each operational period.

Tactics - Deploying and directing resources on an incident to accomplish incident strategy and objectives.

Tank Mix - A mixture of pesticides or pesticides and fertilizers applied at the same time.

Tannerite—a low explosive used for exploding targets consisting of Ammonium Nitrate or Ammonium Perchlorate and aluminum powder. This is shipped in two packages combined on-site. Very insensitive to shock and requires the impact of a rifle bullet to ignite.

TAP - Toxicological Agent Protective (e.g., TAP Apron)

Tare Weight - the weight of the container, wrapper, vehicle, etc. deducted from the total weight to determine the weight of the contents or load.
Wa
Target Organ Effect - Toxins which selectively attack the liver, kidneys, Central Nervous System, eyes, lungs, etc.

TATP- Triacetone Triperoxide—a high explosive used extensively by terrorists due to the simplicity of manufacture which can be done at a kitchen sink.

TCLP-Toxic Characteristic Leaching Program—an analytical procedure to determine soil contamination or to determine if a Waste is a characteristic hazardous waste. Sometimes referred to as a **Toxic Characteristic Leachate Profile**

Termination - that portion of incident management in which personnel are involved in documenting safety procedures, site operations, hazards faced, and lessons learned from the incident. Termination is divided into three phases: debriefing the incident, post incident analysis, and critiquing the incident.

Task Force - Any combination of resources assembled to support a specific mission or operational need. All resource elements within a Task Force must have common communications and a designated leader.

Task Force - A combination of single resources assembled for a particular tactical need with common communications and a Leader.

TBM - Theater Ballistic Missile

TC - Training Circular

TD50 (Toxic Dose) - The dose of a substance needed to produce a defined toxic effect in 50 percent of the exposed population. It is an infrequently used term, equivalent to ED50 where "toxicity" is the measured "effect."

Team - See Single Resource.

Technical Assistance - Support provided to State, local, and tribal jurisdictions when they have the resources but lack the complete knowledge and skills needed to perform a required activity (such as mobile-home park design and hazardous material assessments).

Technical name - Means the recognized chemical name currently used in scientific and technical handbooks, journals, and texts.

Technical Specialists - Personnel with special skills that can be used anywhere within the ICS organization.

TECP Suit - Totally encapsulating chemical protective suit. Special protective suits made of material that prevents toxic or corrosive substances or vapors from coming in contact with the body. Gas and vapor tight suit.

Temperature of the Product – temperature of the material in the shipping container as it is being transported or stored in a container.

Tepid- moderately warm; lukewarm

Teratogen - An agent or substance that may cause physical defects in the developing embryo or fetus when a pregnant female is exposed to that substance.

Teratogenic- tending to produce anomalies of formation or development of the offspring of persons exposed to chemicals

Terrorism - Under the Homeland Security Act of 2002, terrorism is defined as activity that involves an act dangerous to human life or potentially destructive of critical infrastructure or key resources and is a violation of the criminal laws of the United States or of any State or other subdivision of the United States in which it occurs and is intended to intimidate or coerce the civilian population or influence a government or affect the conduct of a government by mass destruction, assassination, or kidnapping. See Section 2 (15), Homeland Security Act of 2002, Pub. L. 107-296, 116 Stat. 2135 (2002).

tert- - An abbreviation for "tertiary". Referring to a particular arrangement of elements within a chemical molecule.

Tetanic - pertaining to or of the nature of tetanus, a disease characterized by muscle spasm
.

Th50 or ThCt50 - The vapor dosage producing the defined threshold (low-level) response in 50 percent of the given population. Within the context of this Glossary, the route of exposure can be either inhalation or percutaneous.

THAAD - Theater High Altitude Area Defense

Thermal Energy - The energy emitted from the fireball as thermal radiation. The total amount of thermal energy received per unit area at a specified distance from a nuclear explosion is generally expressed in terms of calories per square centimeter.

Thermal Radiation - Electromagnetic radiation emitted (in two pulses from an air burst) from the fireball as a consequence of its very high temperature; it consists essentially of ultraviolet, visible, and infrared radiations. In the early stages (first pulse of an air burst), when the temperature of the fireball is very high, the ultraviolet predominates; in the second pulse, the temperatures are lower and most of it is in the visible and infrared regions of the spectrum.

Thermonuclear - An adjective referring to the process in which very high temperatures are used to bring about the fusion of light nuclei (hydrogen), with the accompanying liberation of energy. A thermonuclear bomb is a weapon in which part of the explosion energy results from thermonuclear fusion reactions. The high temperatures required are obtained by means of a fission explosion.

Thermonuclear weapon - A nuclear weapon in which fusion of light nuclei, such as deuterium and tritium, contributes the main explosive energy. The high temperatures required for such fusion reactions are obtained by means of an initial fission explosion. It is also referred to as a hydrogen bomb.

Thio- - Containing a sulfur atom.

TP Triphosgene, also called trichloromethyl carbonate. A pulmonary agent similar to phosgene. The decomposition products of TP include phosgene. Triphosgene has been used as an industrial intermediate but its use is limited by the serious toxicity issues.

Transport Index – For Radioactive materials in transport--The dimensionless number, rounded up to the first decimal place, placed on the label of a package to designate the degree of control to be exercised by the carrier during transportation. The transport index is the number expressing the maximum radiation level in millirem per hour at 1 meter from the external surface of the package.

Threat - An indication of possible violence, harm, or danger.

Threshold - The lowest dose of a chemical at which a specific measurable effect is observed. Below this dose, the effect is not observed.

Threshold Dose - The smallest amount of toxic substance that can produce the first recognizable injuries (e.g., irritation of skin, eyes, or nose; miosis).

Threshold Limit Value - Ceiling (TLV-C) - The concentration in air that should not be exceeded during any part of the working exposure. Ceiling limits may supplement other limits or may stand alone.

Threshold Limit Value, TLV - Estimate of the average concentration of a toxic substance that can safely be tolerated over an 8 or 12 hour work day. TLV values are recommendations of the ACGIH. Note that TLVs do not have the force of law except in jurisdictions where the law incorporates them by reference.

Threshold Limit Value/Short Term Exposure (TLV/STEL) - The 15-minute time weighted average exposure which should not be exceeded at any time, nor repeated more than four times daily with a 60 minute rest period between each STEL exposure. Those short term exposures can be tolerated without suffering irritation, chronic or irreversible tissue damage, or narcosis of a sufficient degree to increase the likelihood of accidental injury, impairing self-rescue, or reducing worker efficiency. TLV/STEL are expressed in either ppm or mg/m3.

Threshold Limit Value/Time Weighted Average (TLV/TWA) - The maximum Airborne concentration of a material to which an average healthy person may be repeatedly exposed for eight hours each day , forty hours each week, without suffering adverse effects. TLV/TWA are expressed in either ppm or mg/m3.

Thrombocytopenia - An absolute decrease in the circulating platelets in the blood.

TICs—Toxic Industrial Chemicals

Tidal volume - amount of gas that is inhaled and exhaled during one respiratory cycle

TIM - toxic industrial material

Time Unit - Functional Unit within the Finance/Administration Section responsible for recording time for incident personnel and hired equipment.

Tinnitus - a noise in the ears, such as ringing, buzzing, roaring, clicking

Title III - The third part of SARA, also known as the Emergency Planning and Community Right-to-Know Act of 1986.

TLV - Threshold Limit Values see Threshold Limit Values

TMD - Theater Missile Defense

TOC - Total Organic Content measured in ppm for organics in water.

TOFC - Trailer-on-Flatcar

Tolerance - The ability to endure the effects of a pesticide or pest without exhibiting adverse effects.

Tools - Those instruments and capabilities that allow for the professional performance of tasks, such as information systems, agreements, doctrine, capabilities, and legislative authorities.

Toxic - Capable of causing human injury. A poison. Pertaining to, due to, or of the nature of a poison.

Toxic Materials - A type of chemical that can cause chemical harm at an incident scene. They produce harmful effects depending on the concentration of the materials and the length of exposure to them. An individual can have chronic or acute exposures to toxic materials.

Toxic Products of Combustion – Materials produced during a fire that can cause human injury. These materials are compounds such as carbon monoxide, hydrogen cyanide, acrolein, hydrochloric acid, soot, and ash

Toxin - a poisonous substance produced during the metabolism and growth of certain microorganisms and some higher plant and animal species. A toxin (Greek: toxikon) is a poisonous substance produced by living cells or organisms. Man-made substances created by artificial processes usually aren't considered toxins by this definition.

Toxicity - The degree of danger posed by a substance to animal or plant life. The potential a pesticide has for causing harm.

Toxicology - The study of the adverse effects of chemicals on biological systems, and the assessment of the probability of their occurrence.

Toxicological Effects –
   a. **Additive**--Situation in which the combined effect of two chemicals is equal to the sum of the effect of each agent given alone (e.g., 2+3=5). :
   b. **Synergistic**—Situation in which the combined effect of two chemicals is much greater than the sum of the effect of each agent given alone (e.g., 2+3=20). :
   c. **Potentiation**--Situation in which one substance does not have a toxic effect, but when it is added to another chemical, it makes the latter much more toxic (e.g., 0+3=10).
   d. **Antagonism**--Situation in which two chemicals given together interfere with each other's actions or one interferes with the action of the other

chemical (e.g., 4+6=8, 4+0=1, 4+4=0).

TRACEM - The acronym used to identify the six types of harm one may encounter at a terrorist incident: **T**hermal, **R**adioactive, **A**sphyxiation, **C**hemical, **E**tiological, and **M**echanical.

Tracking Powder - A fine powder that is dusted over a surface to detect or control certain pests such as cockroaches or rodents. For control, the inert powder is combined with a pesticide; the animal ingests this powder and becomes poisoned when it cleans itself.

Trade name - The commercial name or trademark by which a chemical is known. One chemical may have a variety of trade names depending on the manufacturers or distributors involved.

trans- - Referring to a particular arrangement of elements within a chemical molecule.

Transformation - The chemical alteration of a compound by processes such as reaction with other compounds or breakdown into component elements.

Transport - Hydrological, atmospheric, or other physical processes that convey pollutants through and across media from source to receptor.

Tribal - Any Indian tribe, band, nation, or other organized group or community, including any Alaskan Native Village as defined in or established pursuant to the Alaskan Native Claims Settlement Act (85 Stat. 688) (43 U.S.C.A. and 1601 et seq.), that is recognized as eligible for the special programs and services provided by the United States to Indians because of their status as Indians.

Trichothecene Mycotoxins - A diverse group of more than 40 compounds produced by fungi. They are potent inhibitors or protein synthesis, impair DNA synthesis, alter cell membrane structure and function, and inhibit mitochondrial respiration. Secondary metabolites of fungi, such as T-2 toxin and others, produce toxic reactions called mycotoxicoses upon inhalation or consumption of contaminated food products by humans or animals.

Triglyceridemia - excess of triglycerides in the blood

TSWG - Technical Support Working Group

Tularemia - A zoonotic disease caused by Francisella tularensis, a gram-negative bacillus. Humans acquire the disease under natural conditions through inoculation of skin or mucous membranes with blood or tissue fluids of infected animals, or bites of infected deerflies, mosquitoes, or ticks.

Type - A classification of resources in the ICS that refers to capability. Type 1 is generally considered to be more capable than Types 2, 3, or 4, respectively, because of size; power; capacity; or, in the case of incident management teams, experience and qualifications.

U

UAV - Unmanned Aerial Vehicle

UC - Unified Command

UEL, UFL - The upper flammable limit (UFL) or upper explosive limit (UEL) is the maximum vapor to air concentration above which propagation of a flame will not occur.

Ultra-Low Volume (ULV) - A pesticide application technique in which very small amounts of liquid spray are applied over a unit of area; usually 1/2 gallon or less of spray per acre in row crops to about 5 gallons of spray per acre in orchards and vineyards.

UN - United Nations

UN Identification Number - An international four digit number assigned to all hazardous materials regulated by the United Nations.

Unified Area Command - A Unified Area Command is established when incidents under an Area Command are multijurisdictional. (See Area Command.)

Unified Command - An application of ICS used when there is more than one agency with incident jurisdiction or when incidents cross political jurisdictions. Agencies work together through the designated members of the Unified Command, often the senior person from agencies and/or disciplines participating in the

Unified Command, to establish a common set of objectives and strategies and a single Incident Action Plan.

Unit - The organizational element having functional responsibility for a specific incident Planning, Logistics, or Finance/Administration activity.

Unity of Command - The concept by which each person within an organization reports to one and only one designated person. The purpose of unity of command is to ensure unity of effort under one responsible commander for every objective.

Unsaturated Hydrocarbon – a hydrocarbon that contains on carbon and hydrogen, but has double bonds or triple bonds. Hydrocarbons that have double or triple covalent bonds between adjacent carbon atoms. Those with at least one double bond are called alkenes and those with at least one triple bond are called alkynes. Alkenes with two double bonds are called dienes.

UNSCOM - UN Special Commission on Iraq

UNSCR - UN Security Council Resolution

Unstable - A chemical is unstable if it tends to decompose or undergo other undesirable chemical changes during normal handling or storage.

Upper Explosive Limit or Upper Flammable Limit (UEL or UFL) - The concentration of a substance above which an ignition source (flame, spark, etc.) will not create a flame or explosion. Above this level, the air/contaminant mixture is too "rich" to burn (see also LEL/LFL).

Urban Search and Rescue (US&R) Task Force (US&R Team) -Federal asset that conducts physical search and rescue in collapsed buildings; provides emergency medical care to trapped victims; assesses and controls gas, electrical services, and hazardous materials (HazMat); and evaluates and stabilizes damaged structures. *See Annex A: Federal Response Teams for more detailed information on this Federal Resource.*

Urticant - Something that causes itching or stinging and a raised area on the skin (wheal).

Urticaria - a vascular reaction of the skin marked by the transient appearance of smooth, slightly elevated patches (wheals) which are redder or paler than the surrounding skin and often attended by severe itching

US&R - Urban Search and Rescue

USAMRCD - U.S. Army Medical Research and Material Command

USDA - United States Department of Agriculture

V

Vacuolation - Formation of a space.

Vapor - The gaseous form of substances that are normally in the solid or liquid state that can be changed to this state by increasing the pressure or decreasing the temperature. These vapors will diffuse.

Vapor Density - Vapor density is the ratio of the density of any gas or vapor to the density of air, under the same conditions of temperature and pressure. It is a measure of how heavy the vapor is in relation to the same volume of air. A vapor density of 1.0 is equal to air. Vapors that are heavier than air may build up in low-lying areas, such as along floors, in sewers, or in elevator shafts. Vapors that are lighter than air rise and may collect near the ceiling. Vapor density helps in estimating how long an agent will persist in valleys and depressions. The higher the vapor density, the longer the vapor will linger in low-lying areas.

Vapor pressure - Is the pressure exerted by the vapor of a substance in a closed container. It is a measure of a substance's tendency to emit or give off vapors. The higher the vapor pressure, the more volatile the substance, thus the more vapor given off. The lower the boiling point the higher the vapor pressure. Vapor pressure increases with temperature. If a chemical with a high vapor pressure spills, there is an increased risk of explosion and a greater risk that workers will inhale toxic fumes.

Vascularization - Development of new blood vessels in a structure.

Vasoconstriction - Diminution of interior size of a blood vessel with resultant decrease in blood flow.

Vasodilation - dilation (expansion of a vessel, especially of arterioles) leading to increased blood flow to a part.

VCL - Vapor Control Line

Vector - An organism such as an insect that can transmit a pathogen to plants or animals.

VEE - Venezuelan equine encephalomyelitis

Vent and Burn - The use of shaped explosive charges to vent the high pressure at the top of a pressurized container and then, with additional charges, release and burn the remaining liquid in the container in a controlled fashion. This is a highly sophisticated technique that is only used under very controlled conditions.

Ventricular fibrillation - irregular heart beat characterized by uncoordinated contraction of the ventricle

Vertebrate - The group of animals that haven an internal skeleton and segment spine, such as fish, birds, reptiles and mammals.

Vertigo - dizziness; an illusion of movement as if the external world were revolving around an individual or as if the individual were revolving in space

Very Flammable - In this volume, defined as the equivalent of NFPA Flammability Hazard Class 2.

Vesicant - Causing blisters or vesicles.

Vesicants - Chemical agents, also called blister agents, which cause severe burns to eyes, skin, and tissues of the respiratory tract. Also referred to as mustard agents, examples include mustard and lewisite.

Vesicating Agent - Agent which acts on the eyes and lungs and blisters the skin.

Vesication - The process of blistering.

Vibrio cholerae- The biological agent causing cholera

Viral Hemorrhagic Fevers - A diverse group of human viral illnesses characterized by acute febrile onset accompanied by headache and complicated by increased vascular permeability, damage, and bleeding; mortality is high. Examples include Rift Valley Fever, Ebola Hemorrhagic Fever, and Yellow Fever.

Virus - Any of various submicroscopic pathogens consisting essentially of a core of a single nucleic acid surrounded by a protein coat, having the ability to replicate only inside a living cell.

Viscosity - Measure of the thickness of a liquid and will determine its ease of flow. Liquids with high viscosity, such as heavy oils, have to be heated to increase their fluidity.

VOC – Volatile Organic Compound

Volatile - readily vaporizable at a relatively low temperature. Able to pass from liquid into a gaseous stage readily.

Volatility - Describes the ease or rate that a liquid or solid can pass into the vapor state. The higher the volatility, the greater the rate of evaporation. Volatility is the weight of vapor present in a unit volume of air, under equilibrium conditions, at a specified temperature. It is a measure of how much material (agent) evaporates under given conditions. The volatility depends on vapor pressure. It varies directly with temperature. We express volatility as milligrams of vapor per cubic meter (mg/m3). Calculate it numerically by an equation derived from the perfect gas law.

Volatilization - Entry of contaminants into the atmosphere by evaporation from soil or water

Volunteer - For purposes of the NIMS, a volunteer is any individual accepted to perform services by the lead agency, which has authority to accept volunteer services, when the individual performs services without promise, expectation, or receipt of compensation for services performed. See, e.g., 16 U.S.C. 742f(c) and 29 CFR 553.101.

VX - a nerve agent; ethyl-S-dimethylaminoethyl methylphosphonothiolate

W

Warm zone - Area where personnel and equipment decontamination and hot zone support take place. It includes control points for the access corridor and thus assists in reducing the spread of contamination. Also referred to as the decontamination, contamination reduction, or limited access zone in other documents. (NFPA 472)

Warning - The signal word used on labels of pesticides in toxicity Category II, having an oral LD50 between 50 and 500 and a dermal LD50 between 200 and 2000.

Water reactivity - Describes the sensitivity of materials to water without requiring heat or confinement.

Water solubility - Provides information on the degree to which a substance is soluble in water.

Water spray (fog) - Method or way to apply or distribute water. The water is finely divided to provide for high heat absorption. Water spray patterns can range from about 10 to 90 degrees. Water spray streams can be used to extinguish or control the burning of a fire or to provide exposure protection for personnel, equipment, buildings, etc. (This method can be used to absorb vapors, knock-down vapors or disperse vapors. Direct a water spray (fog), rather than a straight (solid) stream, into the vapor cloud to accomplish any of the above). Water spray is particularly effective on fires of flammable liquids and volatile solids having flash points above 37.8°C (100°F). Regardless of the above, water spray can be used successfully on flammable liquids with low flash points. The effectiveness depends particularly on the method of application. With proper nozzles, even gasoline spill fires of some types have been extinguished when coordinated hose lines were used to sweep the flames off the surface of the liquid. Furthermore, water spray carefully applied has frequently been used with success in extinguishing fires involving flammable liquids with high flash points (or any viscous liquids) by causing frothing to occur only on the surface, and this foaming action blankets and extinguishes the fire.

Water-sensitive - Substances which may produce flammable and/or toxic decomposition products upon contact with water.

Waybill - A document for a single railcar that includes shipper and location, consignee and location, car contents, DOT shipping description (if hazardous materials) and amount of shipment (volume or weight). Waybills do not travel with the shipment but can be accessed for specific car information.

Well Car - A flat car with a depression or opening in the center to allow the load to extend below the normal floor level when it could not otherwise come within the overhead clearance limits. Commonly used in double stack intermodal service.

Wheel Burns - Damage to a tank caused by continued contact with a turning wheel. This results in damage to the tank similar to a score but with increased heating at the contact area.

Wheel Flange - The tapered projection extending completely around the inner rim of a railway wheel, the function of which, in conjunction with the flange of a mater wheel, is to keep the wheel set on the track by limiting lateral movement of the assembly against the inside surface of either rail.

WDI - Wood Destroying Insect

WDO - Wood Destroying Organism

Weed - Any undesirable plant; a plant out of place

Wettable Powder - A solid (powder) which is not soluble in water but when added to water will form a suspension.

Wetting Agent - A product which will reduce the surface tension of a liquid, helping it stick to a given surface.

WMD - Weapons of Mass Destruction

Workers Right-to-Know - Legislation mandating communicating of chemical information to employees. A regulatory initiative by OSHA, and an antecedent to Community Right-to-Know.

X

X-Ray - A class of high energy photon, X-rays have wavelengths of 0.012 to 12 nanometers. Not only are X-rays used for medical imaging (when you break your arm an X-ray machine is used to take a picture of the broken bone). Penetrating electromagnetic radiation (photon) having a wavelength that is much shorter than that of visible light. Rays produced by excitation of the electron field around certain nuclei are called characteristic x-rays. In nuclear reactions, it is customary to refer to photon originating in the nucleus as gamma rays, and to those originating in the electron field of the atom as X-rays.

Y

Yellow Fever Virus - A member of the Flavivirus group endemic to South America and Africa transmitted to humans by the Aedes Aegypti mosquito. It is also a viral hemorrhagic fever virus. After a 3 to 6 day incubation period, there is abrupt onset of headache, nausea, vomiting, muscle aches, chills, and fever.

Z

Zone, Contamination Reduction (Warm Zone)

The area between the Exclusion Zone and the Support Zone. This zone contains the personnel decontamination station. This zone may require a lesser degree of personnel protection than the Exclusion Zone. This separates the contaminated area from the clean area and acts as a buffer to reduce contamination of the "clean" area. (U.S. Coast Guard Incident Management Handbook, 2001 edition)

Zone, Exclusion (Hot Zone)

The area immediately around a spill or release and where contamination does or could occur. The innermost of the three zones of a hazardous substances/material incident. Special protection is required for all personnel while in this zone. (U.S. Coast Guard Incident Management Handbook, 2001 edition)

Zone, Support (Cold Zone)

The "clean" area outside of the contamination control line. In this area, equipment and personnel are not expected to become contaminated. Special protective clothing is not required. This is the area where resources are assembled to support the hazardous substances/materials release operations. (U.S. Coast Guard Incident Management Handbook, 2001 edition)

Zoonosis - A disease of animals that may be transmitted to man under natural conditions.

Zoonotic - Transmissible from animals to man under natural conditions; pertaining to or constituting a zoonosis.

Zootoxin - A toxin or poison of animal, such as the venom of snakes, spiders, and scorpions.

Common Conversions

Small Drips	Big Drips	ml	English
5000	2500	250	1 cup
10000	5000	500	1 pint
21000	11500	1000	1 quart
75000	38000	3800	1 gallon

Small Drip = 1/20 ml   Big Drip = 1/10 ml

Pressure -- 1 Atmosphere = 760 mm Hg = 407" water = 14.7 psi = 101 kPa

1 bar = 14.5 psi

Temperature conversions

$$°C = 5/9 \ (°F -- 32)$$

$$°F = 9/5 \ (°C) + 32$$

Interconverting PPM and mg/m3

To convert mg/m3 to ppm ppm= (mg/m3)X(24.45) /(MW)

Where 24.45 is a constant representing roughly the molar volume of any gas and MW is the molecular weight of the agent.

Estimating Vapor Density

To calculate the vapor density, divide the MW by 29 (the average MW of air). If the result is greater than 1.0, the agent is heavier than air. The agent will tend to collect in low-lying areas, such as foxholes and ditches, and in vehicles. If the result is less than 1.0, the agent almost invariably is non-persistent. It will quickly dissipate into the atmosphere. For example, phosgene, $COCl_2$, with an MW of 98.92, has a vapor density of 3.4 times that of air. The calculation follows -

Vapor	Molecular Weight	Vapor Density
Phosgene	98.92	3.4
Air	29	1